SUPER CHILD

SUPER CHILD

52 Habits of Parenting

(One Habit Each Week)

Rohit Mehra (IRS)

Published by
PRABHAT PRAKASHAN PVT. LTD.
4/19 Asaf Ali Road,
New Delhi-110 002 (INDIA)
e-mail: prabhatbooks@gmail.com

ISBN 978-93-89982-41-1
SUPER CHILD
by Shri Rohit Mehra (IRS)

Edition
2025

Price
₹ 250.00 (Rupees Two Hundred Fifty only)

Printed at
Narula Printers, Delhi

Dedicated to all the parents
who strive to give best to their
children and wants to unleash the
true potential of their children by
imbibing best of the best habits,
and values in them.

Preface

As per Socrates 99% of what we do, think and feel is habits. Even modern research says that 45 % of what we do is our habits. Habits are what we are. First we make habits then habits make us! So, it becomes all the more important to make habits during the formative and growing years of our children's physical, mental and emotional personality. Parents want best of their children. Over the years, I have found that there is a missing gap between what we as parents aspire our children to be and the habits needed by them to reach to those aspirations. This book tries to fill this gap.

Further, I have also found that there is a gap between what children are taught in our modern education system and what their practical life is. The purposes of education are two a) to teach the child how to make his living b) to teach the child how to live life. It is jokingly said that those who are back-benchers (who are less serious in classrooms) perform better in life than those who are front-benchers. The purpose of every learning course is a cause. Children learn language so as to be better communicators, they learn science so as they can co-relate cause and effect, they learn history so as to learn culture and past-mistakes, so and so forth. Parents are more led by competition, marks, grades and promising career. These parts of formal education are no doubt needed and need of the time. But, many a times out education system misses the link between the purposes of learning and needs of our modern education-system of grades and scores. This book is an attempt to fill this missing link.

Besides learning different tools and subjects and preparing the child for the competitive world, education has one determining purpose. This purpose of education is so obvious, but sadly it is often underrated, missed or even does not figure out in the minds and hearts of parents and teachers. We as parents try to live our dreams, wishes and aspiration through our children. Modern education system tries to teach the child what the society knows as collective wisdom. Every child is born with uniqueness. Most parents live their life through their child, but this book will help them to bring out what is best in their child. The purpose of education is not to teach the child what we as society know but to bring out what the child knows. The purpose of education is to unleash the true potential of your child. Simply, it is teaching him how to live life. This book will help you as parents to find out the true purpose and potential of your child. Having found the true potential of your child, this book will help you to teach your child some of the simplest yet highly rewarding habit so as your child can achieve his true potential in an effective yet easy manner.

To develop all round personality of your child which includes its variants viz, physical, mental, emotional and spiritual aspects; child needs specific and measureable habits to achieve them. I have given a detail of 52 effective habits (which habits to follow), common benefits of a particular habit (why these habits needed to be followed), and simplest way to make habits (how to make these habits). For example, it is universally accepted that child should eat a fruit per day. Every parent tells their child to have a fruit. Even the school curriculum has a full chapter on benefits on eating fruits. But, the percentage of children who eat fruit per day in India is as less as 20%! So, this book will teach him how he can make a habit of eating a fruit thereby filling the gap between what is taught and what is needed.

This book tries to answer questions like: How to make habits which make your child not only efficient but effective also? What are the factors in making life long habits which stay? Not only which habits are to be developed but how to make habits and what are the benefits of each habit. What is the simplest and easiest way to make and sustain habits? What is the role of parents as well as family environment in shaping the habits of the child? How to involve yourself in making habits of your child? What is the role of accountability partner so as if the child has siblings, they all can make habits together by working for each other. How to overcome entrenched bad habits? I have experimented some of few productive habits with my own two lovely children. I must say that when it is making of any habit, they outsmart me and my wife. They have an amazing potential to learn and apply. We have just to be the right trigger.

Further, research also suggests that children are the best observers. They do not do what we tell them to do or not to do. They do what they observe in their parents. They copy and imitate our manners, habit and values. So, we as parents are their role-models as we influence them a lot. In the process of making their habits, we will surely make our own habits.

We want best of our Children. You can make your Child a Super-Child! Yes, you heard it right. Habits are the way which can really make our Child super-Child. It is super-child by Habits. Our child needs good habits, skills and values which he can make to develop himself in to a super-child and unleash his true potential. This book is based on this theme. There are 52 simple habits which correspond to 52 weeks in a year. Child can make 1 habit per week and by the end of the year, he is having 52 habits which will surely make him super-child.

The various chapters in this book consist of behaviours, manners, skills, habits and values which a child must possess so as he can be what he should be in life. These 52 habits cover all the aspects of child's life be it is his health, hygiene and fitness; his academics, his passions and purposes, his belief-system, his personal and family values. By reading this book, he as well as his parents can help him find his passion and purpose of life and how to successfully achieve them by adopting these 52 habits.

Ps: The book has used *him* as a word to refer the child which means her also. Also, word child has been used singularly which connotes children also.

What are Habits and How are They Formed?

Habits are those processes, behaviors and actions which we repeat subconsciously on a daily basis. They are necessary for the functioning of human-beings. If we don't have habits, we have to consciously decide even the smallest of smallest action. Imagine for instance, daily you have to think of reason of why and how to brush, exercise, bath, drive your car, use your mobile etc. As per the latest research on human-brain, our brain has two parts: (a) The one part is active and conscious and is the place where decision are made based on logic and reason, the 'decision-making brain'. We often call it as 'conscious-brain'. (b) Another part is old and is comparatively less active and is the store house of all our emotions, memories and 'pattern-recognition'. We call this the 'subconscious-brain'. When we repeat something consistently, that action or behavior gets registered as a pattern in subconscious-part of brain and is stored in the *'basal-ganglia'*. This *'basal-ganglia'* is the store house of patterns which come-out when there is a trigger which activates that behavior. *'Basal-ganglia'* helps brain to repeat the pattern or behavior automatically without any 'conscious decision making'. The moment this pattern-recognition part is activated, our brain is overtaken by this part. We behave and act as per the dictates of this part of the brain which supersedes rationality, logic or even emotions. It is on automatic-mode. For example, when the habit of smoking is triggered, the brain craves for it forgetting the consequences of smoking. Even the doctors, who know much more than a common man the health hazards of cigarette, succumb to the habit of smoking!

Why Habits are Necessary

Habits are necessary as they save time and energy of the brain. Otherwise, every time the brain has to consciously decide why and how of any action or behavior. Habits they help the brain to focus on other areas while they take care of their areas automatically. They save energy of the brain. It takes too much of energy of the brain when it takes part in 'decision-making' process. Habit based action are independent of the current mood, state of mind and level of motivation an individual is going through. There is no limit to the number of habits one can follow! Hence, habit based action may be limitless. Man is the sub-total of the habits he has!

How to Make Habits

You can be the architect of your habits instead of being their victim. There is a simple way of habit-forming which is known as habit-loop. Three things are must to form a habit: trigger, behaviour and reward. For example, alarm goes off and you get up, you crave for a cup of tea, you feel rewarded with the taste of tea and feel active. This process happens repeatedly even without even you thinking of it! This becomes a habit loop. James Clear in his Atomic Habits includes four steps to make a habit. To transform a behavior in to a habit, the behaviour must be obvious, attractive, easy and satisfying. And to stop a bad habit, it must be made invisible, unattractive, difficult and unsatisfying. For example, if you keep a fruit in your bedroom, the chances of you eating that fruit goes 90 % up than you getting up, going to fetch fruit from kitchen and eating up. It is a classic example of habits made easy and obvious.

One of the other ways to make habits is stacking. If you have any current habit, stack the new desired action before that habit. For example, I made my habit of drinking more water by stacking my habit like this: Before sitting on my chair in office in the morning, I will drink a glass of water. This way I could make my habit of drinking enough water. One of the best ways to make and sustain habits is by rewarding yourself for the completion of the desired habit: Browsing Facebook, only after you have read 2 pages of a book. This is the easiest way which will help you make the habit of reading.

Let's venture to make our child, a Super-child.

Acknowledgement

I am blessed by the almighty who has shown me my passions of life and the way how to bring out that passion for the betterment of others. I am eternally indebted to my grandfather, late Sh. Ram Prakash Mehra who has influenced me a lot and has imbibed in me such values and sanskaras which have helped me in becoming what I am. I cannot thank enough my father, Sh. Rajesh Mehra and my mother, Smt. Parveen who have given me constant love and affection. Many of the habits given in the book have been parented by them.

I have got constant support of my love, my wife Geetanjali who has stood by me through my entire journey. I am indebted to her as she managed household and also performed many of the duties of a 'father' so well that I can have enough time to focus on my passions. She has been kind enough to even accept my point of view. My lovely kids, Dhruv and Udhay have been the blessings of my life. I have tried to imbibe most of these habits and values in them by daily practicing with them. We have a score card and reward for each habit in family. I used to narrate every chapter of this book daily at bedtime. I cannot thank my soul-mate, Sundari enough. I have been blessed enough to have inspiring mentors as teachers in my life like, Late Smt. Sumitra Devi, Late Smt. Urmil Puri, Sh. M.K. Sharma, Late Dr. Gurnam Singh, Sh. Santosh Taneja Ji , Sh. Devender Triguna, Sh. B.K. Jha IRS, Sh. Savjibhai and others who have influenced me a lot. A special thanks to Sh. D.S. Chaudhry IRS, Sh. Rajiv Nagpal ji and Sh. Arun Anand Ji. My book would not have been completed without the constant motivation of my friends Rajesh, Rajubhai, Sanjay, Gourav, Sushant, Mohit, Capt. Arya and Anshul. A special thanks to Johny Kapoor, Ashu Bhabi, Pallavi and Madam Smriti. A very special thanks to Mrs. Wilson for editing and guiding. A special thanks to Inder Rawat, Amit and Sarla. The views expressed in this book are purely personal.

Contents

1

Habit of Chewing Food Properly

The biggest asset for a human being is his health. We say health is wealth. We have also heard many times that in a healthy body lives a healthy mind. The most important factor for a healthy body is a healthy and robust digestive system. For our digestive system to be robust, one of the easiest, healthiest and rewarding habits is to masticate food properly. Most children gulp down their food very fast or swallow a meal while working or sitting in front of a television. As per Ayurveda, digestion of food starts from the mouth and not from the stomach. It advises us to chew our food 32 times; wherein 32 times is equal to the number of teeth an adult generally has. When we swallow our food, our digestive system breaks down this food into small parts so that the necessary nutrients are absorbed by the body. If the food is chewed 32 times, even the most solid food gets liquefied and becomes easy to assimilate.

Why do Children Eat Fast?

The habit of eating fast is not one day's result; rather, it is the product of a long time, often starting in childhood. The following may be the reasons:

- An old habit which is developed during early childhood which generally originates from the habit of feeding by the mothers.

- Doing other things while eating food like reading magazine, watching T.V. or browsing mobile, chatting, playing games, etc.
- Urgency of finishing a meal due to the pressure of time, such as going to school or tuition class, or being late to office by the parent.
- Lack of awareness of the benefits of slow eating.
- Disturbance while eating food like a phone call, an argument during a meal or break in a meal.
- Oral issues, like cavity or pain.

Benefits of Masticating Food

- As per science, our saliva in mouth has enzymes which help in making the food alkaline and thus easy to digest. It leads to improved digestive system
- Chewing helps the child to eat mindfully, enjoy the taste of the dish and help absorb all the nutrients present in food.
- Child tends to eat less. When you eat slowly, you tend to eat less but properly. It takes our stomach a couple of minutes to signal our brain that it is already full.
- It prevents obesity in children and strengthens the their immune system leading to good health and longevity. It is a very good exercise for teeth.

How to Build this Habit

- Create awareness from childhood, both at home and in school, on the importance of chewing food properly.
- Start small. Start with the first bite and ask him to chew it 32 times. Tell him to say 'wow' after he has chewed his first bite properly so as to give him some sense of accomplishment. After following this habit for five days, tell him to chew the second bite of each

meal also 32 times. Thereafter, he can increase this habit with other morsels of food.

- Before the child eats his food, tell him to remind himself of this habit. Demonstrate the habit of chewing 32 times by counting loudly at first and then mentally. Gradually counting aloud (7-10 days) can reduce, as by now it would have become a habit.
- If the child has already the habit of eating his food without chewing properly, let him resolve that out of an average of 35 bites in a meal, he will chew at least one morsel 32 times.
- It is up to the parent to encourage meals at the dining-table in a relaxed environment, so that the focus of chewing every morsel becomes a routine, not only for the child, but for all the members of the family.

□

2

Habit of Drinking Enough Water

Science says that the human body is made up of 60 per cent water. So we need a regular intake of water to keep our body hydrated. Research further suggests that our body needs water at regular intervals. Keeping hydrated is vital for health and well-being of the child, though many children do not drink enough water each day. Also, most parents are not aware of the value of taking enough water. This habit is not in their list of priorities, either for themselves or for their children. Such is the importance of drinking water at regular intervals that many schools have started a water-bell just to remind the children to drink water!

Habit

Consuming enough water is necessary so that the body remains hydrated. There is not universally agreed quantity of daily intake of water. However, the minimum required quantity as per latest research is 8 glasses of water per day.

Benefits

- Keeps the body of the child hydrated.
- Lubricates the joints, forms saliva and mucus and circulates oxygen throughout the body. Water

regulates the body temperature and helps maintain the blood pressure.

- Helps the internal organs of body to function properly.
- Boosts the health and beauty of the skin.
- Helps in detoxifying the unwanted and waste products from the body.
- Drinking enough water gives constant energy at regular intervals throughout the day.

When and How to take Water

As per Ayurveda, one should consume at least one to two glasses of water kept overnight in a copper vessel after getting up daily in the morning. A child should drink water throughout the day at regular intervals. Water must be taken while sitting, instead of standing as the latter may damage the joints of the lower parts of the body in the long run. Water should be consumed in small sips, instead of in one shot, and instead of cold water, tepid water is recommended. Intake of water is prohibited immediately after eating a meal since it slows down the digestive fire. Water can be taken only after 45 minutes of consuming food. Also, intake of water should be curbed just before sleep.

Developing this Habit

- Keep a copper vessel filled with water at the bedside of the child. The moment he gets up, make him drink a glass of water. This will not only make him feel fresh but also clear his stomach.
- Always have a fresh water jar filled with fresh vegetables kept on the table of the child. This will work as a trigger for him to drink water.

- Replace soda and cold drink with water or fresh fruit juices. In the beginning, if the child gets addicted to fizzy drinks, give him such a drink only after he has taken a glass of fresh juice in the day.
- Make him carry a water-bottle with him to school or for playing.

□

3

Habit of Adopting Correct Body Posture

Do you know the first thing you notice when you meet someone is his or her posture? Such is the impact of posture that it defines the personality of a child. Having a correct posture not only defines the physical aspect of the child's personality but mental and social aspects as well. Most children have the habit of being sloppy or slouching or standing in a bent posture which is an incorrect way to carry yourself. Have you come across any model, sportsman or actor who has a slouching or stooped posture? I bet you have not. Just observe a soldier. The soldier carries a correct body posture which makes him appear active, smart and attractive. The posture is the most underrated aspect which is vital for the child's overall well-being and leading him a pain-free life.

Habit

What is the correct posture?

Posture is the position in which we hold our bodies while standing, sitting, or lying down. A good posture entails holding the body in its natural state with correct alignment. This means maintaining the shoulder pulled up, back straight and neck elongated.

Benefits

- Makes the child look smart, active and confident.

- Keeps the body of the child flexible, agile and healthy.
- As per research, sleeping in the correct posture helps the child to gain height.
- In the long run, the bones and joints of the child's body remain agile.
- Protect the child from future posture-related complications, like back or neck pain, cervical etc.

Maintaining a Correct Body Posture

- Carry yourself with a correct body posture so that the child observes and follows you.
- The best way to correct the posture of the child is to stand with the back of his head against the wall. Tell your child to check his posture immediately after taking a bath in the bathroom, so that it becomes a part of his daily routine.
- Make him accountable not only for himself but also for his siblings or other family members wherein he checks and point-out their posture by guiding them or giving them tips to maintain an erect posture.
- Make the child follow the posture of his role model like a cricketer, actor or an army man.

□

4

Healthy Toilet Habits

One of the simplest yet important habits which every parent should imbibe in his child is healthy toilet habits and to use the toilet in a proper manner. Correct toilet habits is a basic human body function and a life-skill. It is one of the most important health habits that can have a far-reaching impact on the health of the child. As per Ayurveda, 90 per cent of diseases emanate from the stomach ills which are directly related to unhealthy toilet habits. Disregarding toilet urges can lead to long-term bowel and bladder abnormalities in children. It is better to start toilet habits at an early age.

Habit

Toilet habits are very individualistic. Each child has specific needs and while imparting toilet training to him, one must observe closely and attend to it individually. Simply speaking it is to clear the bowel and bladder first thing in the morning.

Benefits

- Healthy toilet habits are the first condition of healthy stomach which is the basis of healthy and vibrant body.
- A day of vitality, freshness and freedom.
- Freedom from the urge of going to toilet time and again.

- A long-term healthy and disease-free body. A body better suited to growth.
- Personal hygiene.
- Facilitates prevention of many diseases like bladder dysfunction and U.T.I.s (Urinary Tract Infection), constipation and other related diseases.

What and How of Toilet habits

Healthy toilet habits include:

- Teach a child to sit/stand at the pot for natural urges in a proper way.
- Teaching child to obey urges promptly. Teaching child not to withhold a bowel or bladder movement. Teaching your child how to empty his bowels without straining.
- Don't ask children to restrict their habit of drinking water at school. Encourage them to visit the school toilet during break time and not control themselves, till they return home.
- Wash/wipe body organs properly after children have emptied their bowels. Teach them to maintain perennial hygiene.
- Teach children to flush the toilet properly after use and to leave the facility clean after use.
- Practice hand wash after using the toilet.
- Put sanitary napkins in separate paper packs and then bin it.
- Some children, having an imagined fear of monsters/ bugs coming out of the washroom, develop an irrational fear of going to a toilet alone in an unknown place. Teach the child to go to a toilet at other places too, apart from home.
- They should avoid using mobile or any other gadgets in the toilet.

□

5

Healthy Bathroom Habits

One of the basic habits to be imparted to children is healthy bathroom habit. This is a must for a healthy and disease-free child. There are many popular bathroom habits which are used by children but I would try to cite some ignored, yet essential, bathroom habits.

Habit

Bathroom habits include basic habits of body cleaning which are a must for a clean and healthy body of the child. These include brushing the teeth, cleaning the tongue, massaging the face, wiping the body properly, applying perfume and lotion and cleaning the bathroom after use.

Benefits of Healthy Bathroom Habits

- Make the child healthy and clean.
- Increase the overall sanitation and cleanliness of the house.
- Make him self-reliant and independent as far as bathroom use is concerned.
- Teach the child to become more organised.

How to Inculcate Bathroom Habits

Clean the tongue: As per Ayurveda, all toxins accumulate on the tongue. So, besides brushing, cleaning of tongue is very important for overall health of the child besides maintaining his oral health. The child should be taught to clean his tongue with a tongue cleaner from back to forth. He may also use the back of the brush for this purpose. Let this habit be combined with brushing of teeth.

Face massage with oil: It is one of the simplest yet profound habits which will cater to the health of the facial skin of the child for long. Just after brushing, the child should massage his face for one minute with coconut oil or any good skin lotion. If he does not like oil, he may be told that he would be taking a bath anyway which would remove the oil.

Putting water first on foot while bathing: As per Ayurveda, while bathing, one should first pour water on the feet so as to stabilise the internal metabolism of the body and subsequently pour water over the whole body. Modern science corroborates that many of the heart attacks can be prevented through this small habit.

Wipe the body properly: Make him wipe his body completely, including the not-so-easily inaccessible parts, like upper and middle back, inner-thigh, armpit etc. so that he can dry up his body properly.

Wipe bathroom after use: The habit of cleaning the bathroom after it has been used is helpful in maintaining the sanitation of the bathroom. It will save anyone using the bathroom from slipping on a wet floor and help observe a general cleanliness.

Perfume and Lotion: Let these two things be a part of bathroom kits, so that the child can use them immediately after taking the bath.

Prepare a travelling bathroom kit: Make the child prepare a bathroom kit for travelling so as he can habituate this practice. It may include his soap, lotion, brush and other toiletries.

☐

6

Habit of Daily Oiling of the Body

One of the simplest yet very healthy habits in the long run is the habit of oiling our body. When a new-born baby is a month old, the mother nourishes the body of the child by giving gentle oil massages. As per Ayurvedic texts, we should massage our body daily. It is so simple that it takes only less than five minutes to get into this habit. The benefits of oiling the body are many and are not only confined to physical health but mental health and overall vitality and well-being of the child.

Habit

Oiling the body has two aspect:

(a) Massaging the body with oil.

(b) Applying cream or moisturiser on face.

Benefits

- Improves blood circulation and stimulates the internal organs. It strengthens the bones of the child.
- Improves eyesight and also the colour and texture of the skin.
- Helps in rebuilding the body after the wear and tear.
- Increases resistance to disharmony and disease.
- It relaxes the child and removes fatigue. It promotes deeper and better sleep.

- Curbs the speed of ageing. It facilitates vitality and longevity of the body.
- Applying cream on the face helps to nourish the skin of the face, protects the skin from over-exposure to sunlight and keeps the skin hydrated. It slows down the aging of skin and prevents wrinkles and sagging of skin.

Types of Oil and Cream

There are various products in the market. Latest scientific evidence suggests coconut oil to be a good choice, both as an oil as well as face-oil. It is good to read up the contents that go into the manufacture of the cream. Sunscreens are effective during summers and an extra creamy moisturiser is helpful during winters. Another tip is to rely on age-specific creams rather than trying to use the same cream or moisturiser for the family. Creams that enhance fairness and anti-tanning, can be used by teenagers and older people, but should never be used for children, as it can damage the tender skin.

When and how of Oiling and Massage

As per Ayurveda, we should oil our body in the morning before taking a bath. It prescribes that we should rub warm oil over the head and body. Gentle, daily oil massage of the scalp can bring calmness as well as prevent headache, baldness, greying, and receding hairline. It further prescribes use of long, back-and-forth strokes on the long bones in arms and legs, but circular motions over the joints, heart and stomach. Finally, massage the bottoms of the feet. Oiling the body before bedtime will induce sound sleep and keep the skin soft.

New point after the child has taken his bath, let him apply a cream or a moisturiser on his face and other exposed parts of the skin, like neck, elbow and forearms. Cream may also be applied on the legs and feet. The best time to gently massage in the cream is after a bath, either in the morning or at night.

- Make him apply oil on his scalp and body and have a sun bath every fortnight. In winter, this exercise can be done every weekend.

□

7

Habit of Exercise

We take care of our body as it is the only place where we live! As per the definition given in ancient Indian texts, which has now been adopted by even WHO, health is not mere absence of disease (dis-ease) but it is the vitality, vigour and happiness of both the body and mind. Health of a child has two components i.e. food and physical activity. The digital world of Facebook, Twitter, Snapchat, Instagram, Netflix have promoted a sedentary lifestyle and limited their physical movements and activities. Ironically, this generation of children is physically far less active than their previous generations. Exercise is equally important as are academics. Your child's health is more important than his grades. We, as parents, must inculcate the habit of physical activities in children in the form of dancing, cycling, sports, swimming, nature walk, yoga or walking etc-.

Habit of Exercise

Exercise is a bodily activity which makes the body move. It is an activity which enhances physical fitness and overall health and wellness of the body.

Benefits

- Makes the child healthy, fit, agile and active.
- Helps the child gain a good height which is a concern for many parents.

- Helps boost the child's immunity as well as make the child disease free.
- Adding physical activity into your child's daily routine sets the foundation for a lifetime of fitness and good health.
- Motion leads to emotions. It helps him to develop focus and sharpness. Only a good body houses a good mind. If the child has a healthy body, he has a healthy mind.
- Exposing the child to various physical activities may trigger his interests in taking that activity, say sports, as a career.
- Helps in promoting longevity of the child. Research says that those who exercise live longer and have less chances of falling ill.
- If the child does not exercise, his body becomes lethargic. He starts feeling that he is sick and lacks the energy to do anything.
- Acts as an antidote to sitting and becoming a couch potato while watching TV.

Developing the Habit of Physical Activity

- As per research, a child should exercise for a minimum 60 minutes each day which is just 4 % in his time of a day of 24 hours!
- One of the simplest ways to make this a part of child's life is to expose him to various physical, activities including games, dances, yoga, nature, etc. Encourage the child to take part in one or the other sports in the school.
- When exposing the child to various career avenues, do not underrate the value of sports as a career opportunity. Many times, a career in sports is more rewarding than academics. Just see the example of

Ronaldo, Virat Kohli and other sports persons who are much more successful following their career as sportsman.

- Another way is to make the child attend to small household chores which involve physical activity like cleaning up, bringing grocery, make him make his bed as the first thing in the morning etc. Involve the child in minor activities, like gardening or other physical activity.
- One of the simplest ways to make him exercise is to integrate an exercise routine with his favourite hobby. For example, the child can do 10 sit-ups before he turns on the T.V. to watch his favourite programmes.
- Make exercise a family habit and a family value. The entire family should spend at least one hour a week together on any physical activity. Go out for a family walk without the mobile once a week. Also, small family excursions or treks can be organised as often in a year.
- If your apartment has elevators, make your child use the stairs at least for once in day, instead of using the lift. Even if he steps up 200 stairs per day, he has stepped up 73,000 times a year which is 56 kilometers!
- These days most mobiles can be used as health-watches which count the basic parameters, including steps and calories burnt. Use the fitness- data and share your daily steps with your child to promote a healthy competition.
- One of the best exercises for the body is 'Suryanamaskar' (sun-salutation) which is a complete exercise. Make your child do a minimum of five Suryanamaskars each day. It takes just 3 minutes. □

8

Habit to Eat Colourful Food

Health is the greatest blessings we have. This is more so in the case of our growing children. One of the core purposes of parenting is to groom the child to be healthy and disease-free. Health has two components, i.e. food and exercise. The prime constituent of health is food. To bring out the best physical conditions of our children, we, as parents, must develop a habit of making them eat colourful. As per Ayurveda, we are what we eat. Ayurveda says that there are six types of tastes and a healthy meal should consist of all these six tastes and nutrients. Modern science supports this fact. As per a famous study, one of the reasons of people living more than 100 years in 'The Blue Zones' of the world is the habit of eating colourful food! Simply speaking, it is making a habit of eating nutritional as well as varieties of tastes. The five broad component of food are carbohydrates, fat, proteins, vitamins and minerals. Each component is necessary for one or the other functions of the developing body and brain of the child.

Habit

It is making the child eat what is a balanced diet with all the five components in a balanced ratio. It means the child should not only eat tasty food, but healthy food as well.

Benefits

- Helps him intake all the nutrients required for his growth, well-being and health.
- Develops the taste-buds of the child. Helps him cut down on his intake of junk foods.
- Helps to boost his immune system and saves him from any probable illness.
- Helps him adjust and be flexible in all kinds of environment and surroundings. For example, if the child goes for a long weekend or for foreign training or studies, he is more likely to adjust to the food he gets.
- It helps your child to live long and healthy.

Developing this Habit

- Teach your child about all the five prime components of a healthy diet. Also teach them the caloric values of these components and ideal time to eat them. Before eating anything, tell your child all the five components of food.
- Let him make a food audit of what he has eaten in whole day before he sleeps. It should include the junk food as well.
- At least one diet per day should be healthy which should include salad, fruits, nuts and dry-fruits. Make him eat salad with all the meals. Make him eat minimum 2 fruits each day. If he eats too much junk food, stack a few health items with his junk food, like salad before pizza or burger.
- In traditional Indian households children are made to eat leafs of herbs, which, as per research, have many anti-inflammatory and anti-carcinogenic properties. Make him eat one herb per day like *tulsi* (basil), *haldi* (turmeric) etc.

- Make it a family habit to prepare and drink from a jug of alkaline water made with citrus fruit, lemons, *tulsi*, etc. Make every family member, including the child to consume this liquid so that he not only drink alkaline water but essential nutrients along with water.
- The child may also be introduced to herbal tea.

□

9

Habit of Reading Newspaper

Today, we live in an era where information of every kind is easily available at the click of a button. The more you are informed, the more updated you are. 'Reading maketh a man' goes the proverb and the most sensible form of reading and enlightenment is through the positive habit of reading a newspaper. A good routine to develop every morning is the habit of reading the newspaper. In many homes, the first thing that greets you on your doorstep in the morning is the presence of a newspaper. I still remember as a child, the first thing I would do was to bring in the newspaper for my father and he would enjoy reading it, along with his bed tea. He would also make me read the headlines which later on developed into a full-fledged reading habit.

Habit

Simply speaking, it is making the child read the daily news from the newspaper.

Benefits of the Habit of Reading a Newspaper

- True to its acronym, NEWS gives us information from the north, east, west and south. This information covers various fields, such as politics, finance, sports, or international affairs. It is a good source of improving general knowledge apart from keeping him well informed about the happenings across the globe.

- Increases the vocabulary, spelling and reading capacity of a child. It strengthens his writing skills.
- Reading newspapers can kindle his literary interests, like if he is good at writing poems, he can relate to any poem appearing in the newspaper.
- It helps the child understand the practical aspects of academics, for example, in economics, the child is taught about inflation and he can know the current rate of inflation as well as reasons for inflation by reading newspapers.
- Keeps him informed about various career options. It helps him appreciating different viewpoints appearing in different articles and stories. Newspapers can trigger his analytical-mind.
- Reading a newspaper is very useful in various research projects and competitive exams.
- It is less strenuous on the eye and is far better than reading on a mobile.

Developing the Habit of Reading Newspaper

- Subscribe to a newspaper and every morning, before the child has his breakfast, ask him to read the headlines of a newspaper.
- The best way to trigger his interest in academics is to integrate his school learning with newspaper reading. For example, if there is an article on plants, we can tell him to relate this to his botany chapter.
- Ask the child to collect cuttings of news of his interests and make a collage. If he has any role model, e.g. cricket stars, comic strips, cartoons, recipes, fashion, gadgets, encourage him to collect cuttings relating to his interests from the newspaper and paste it in a register.

- On weekends, we can discuss the news of the week and even debate with him on the latest developments and happenings in the country.
- During vacations if there is no holiday homework, we can give him a project on a discussed topic or current topics such as inflation or weather forecast. Ask him to make pie charts, diagrams, flow charts or the details for a fortnight.

□

10

Habit of Conserving Electricity

Small is beautiful. One of the smallest yet simplest habits which most of us do not have is the habit of switching off unnecessary lights and electric equipments which are not in use. This habit is very easy to practice and yet highly rewarding in terms of financial and resource savings.

Habit

Simply speaking this habit requires the child to turn off light or other electric equipments when not required. These lights can be at home, or others' homes, office and public places.

Benefits

- Disciplines the child and triggers the habit of using minimum resources for maximum benefits. It kindles the value of saving in the child which soon spreads to other areas, like saving-water, saving paper, etc.
- Saves electricity and reduces the power bill. The family saves money on electricity bills as it buys light bulbs less often. If you save five units of electricity per day @ ₹6 per unit, you save ₹10,950 per annum. An average Indian family of four members saves

₹43,800 per year! Imagine the national saving if each one of the 130 crore citizens start following this habit.

- Turning lights off will keep a room cooler and an extra benefit in the summer. It reduces electricity usage and extends the life of light bulbs and electronic gadgets Also, it helps in preventing fire as incidents of fire on account of unattended and continued use of electric equipments are very high.
- Saves the national resources as there would be less stress on national resources. By saving electricity, you help in giving electricity to those who do not have access to it.
- Gives the child a better sense of civic culture as saving electricity makes him feel doing something good for the country.
- Helps in improving the health of the child indirectly. Turning off gadgets and T.V. would push the child to go outside in open to play or do something more active.

Building the Habit of Saving Electricity

- A general rule of thumb is that if you or the child is going to be out of the room for 15 minutes or more, turn the lights off.
- Make the child know the cost of electricity and how saving electricity can help the resources and finances of the family and nation, while protecting the environment. Discuss with him the percentage of expenditure on electricity out of the total expenditure for a month. Set a family target to save at least 15 per cent of power-bill in a month. To monitor the habit,

we can compare the monthly bill of our home with the period before forming the habit and after we started this habit.

- Teach the child to look for any light or other electric equipment like fan, air-conditioner, microwave oven, etc. at home or school or public place and turn them off, if not in use.

□

11

Habit of De-clutter

Children of our generations are privileged, especially when it comes to books, toys, stationery, clothes, daily utility items in comparison to our own earlier generation. Many times, our children have much more than they actually require. One of the simplest yet highly effective habits to overcome this 'problem of plenty' is to de-clutter. Simply speaking, it means removing unnecessary stuff from your surroundings and living with only the essential items. De-cluttering is therefore getting rid of those things which are not required in terms of their cost of space, time and finances. If a child were to removes one thing per day, he can de-clutter 365 waste items in a year!

Habit

Removal of unnecessary things and living with minimal required means.

Benefits of De-cluttering

- As the child purposefully de-clutter his school-bag, desk, cupboard, etc., he will realise how much extra stuff he has and starts to evaluate future purchases more carefully. He will buy only the things that he actually requires and uses, and this will ultimately save money as well.
- Creates more space in his bedroom, washroom

or study-table. He will have a better idea of where things are in his home and be able to find them more quickly and easily.

- De-cluttering means lesser belongings to clean, to organise and less stressful to deal with.
- Withdraws the child from non-essentials and focus on the 'essentials'. He can devote greater attention to his passions and other important things of life.
- Makes life simpler by removing unnecessary stuff from the child's life.

Cultivation of This Habit

- Let the child make a list of all the stuff which he uses and classify them under three categories. Items which he is using currently; waste items like old school-books of previous class, discarded-pens, pencils and stationary items, old toys, old clothes, expired coupons, etc. ; and items not required in near future, that is, an item which may not be used in the next six months such as spare toothbrush, stationery, diaries, staplers, etc. Let him collect all the waste items and throw them straight-away in the dustbin. Stuff not required in the near future, say in six months, should be packed in a polythene bag and kept in the storeroom.
- Start with his school bag. He will find many items which are extra and not required. Then let him look at his study table and sports-bag.
- Let him check his wardrobe for clothes not used for the last one year and which he does not require in his life.
- Let him sign in an online buying-selling platform where he can even sell off non-required items. It will help him develop financial-prudency. The best way

is to donate clothes he never wears or gift them to the needy! It will make him learn the value of sharing and gifting.

- The above action of drawing up a list is a one-time affair. Instead, he can set aside 30 minutes in a week to make this habit. Alternatively, he can select daily one item/thing and throw or store it away, which is a better way to create a long-term habit.

□

12

Habit of Maintaining a Dairy

One of the most simple, effective and rewarding habit is the habit of writing a diary every day. It is believed that what can be measured can be achieved and what better way to do so than by recording our thoughts in a diary.

Habit

It is the habit of keeping a personal notebook and jotting down our experiences, emotions, actions every day.

Benefits of Jotting Down Daily Events

- Helps the child to become more expressive and improves his writing and communication skills. The child can express his feelings, be it joy, sorrow, anger, confusion, frustration or happiness.
- When an unpleasant situation or incident in the day is experienced by the child, it is good to record one's feelings instead of venting anger or frustration on others. This habit can work very well to overcome low moods and help the child expresses his suppressed feelings and frustration which is the main reason for depression in children.
- In case of a single child, it is an effective tool to express feelings, without the risk of being betrayed or blackmailed by a friend/confidant. This habit of

journaling can help the child to control his emotions in a positive manner.

- Helps the child to better understand himself. When the child revisits his emotions, after the episode/ event is no longer bothering him, the initial reactions which he had expressed in his diary, if viewed dispassionately, would seem like an overreaction at a later date. When the child grows up, he can revisit the journal and find his personality traits.
- Improves memory and helps the child learn new ideas and concepts. It can trigger creativity and mindfulness in the child.
- In case the child can trust the parent to not be judgemental, he can share his personal space with them. This helps parents know their child better, his expectations, his shortcomings and a host of other critical emotional factors that govern their child.
- Helps to measure his progress. Suppose the child has written a goal that he will exercise for 20 minutes, he can see the next day how far he has achieved his goal. It makes the child accountable.
- Helps him in being better organised and learn what is working or not working in his life.
- Can trigger the child to write a book or autobiography.

Creating the Habit of Journaling

- Buy your child a small dairy. To start with, tell him to write the events of the day, for first few days. Ask him to put a date on each day and sign also. Thereafter, tell him to write down whatever good work he has done in the day. In the next stage he can jot down his wishes, dreams, goals, obstacles, shortcomings, etc. In short, the diary should be a mirror to his soul. After a few days, this simple habit develops into a full-fledged routine. The best time to write a diary is bedtime or early morning, when there is a sense of peace and calm and he can recollect his emotions in serenity. The diary of the child may be kept at his bedside so as he can write daily.

- Make him read autobiographies of great personalities like *My Experiments with Truth* by Mahatma Gandhi. He can see that autobiographies are nothing but personal diaries of great personalities.

□

13

Habit of Watching Motivational Videos

Today we live in the digital world. Our children are exposed to the digital world much more than our generation was as can be seen from their exposure to online-platforms like Google, Facebook, Instagram, Snapchat, YouTube, Netflix or any other online platform. These are the new age ways of reading and browsing content. A new study alerts that children spend more time on YouTube than with their friends. On an average, the child spends a whopping hour and 16 minutes online every day! Exposure to digital-world is an unavoidable realty and is here to stay. In such a scenario, you cannot tell your child to keep away from such gadgets or make him stop using mobiles of other gadgets. The best way to reclaim our children from the ills of digital exposure is to use digital-media for their benefits by guiding them to the positive contents, which will lead to a positive habit formation that is beneficial to them. The best way to use this digital exposure to the advantage of the child is to imbibe in the child a habit of watching motivational videos that are age and content-specific for children.

Habit

It is habit of making the child watch an inspirational or motivational video on digital world daily.

Benefits of the Habit of Watching Motivational Video

- Watching programmes like cartoons or playing online games, or watching stories on Netflix exposes children to many undesirable items that can lead to all kinds of ills. Instead, watching motivational videos helps the child to develop a purpose to life and life goals.
- It exposes the child to new ideas, belief systems and world-view. It gives in a nutshell, the key points in the life of a successful person.
- Watching a video is even better than reading a book in some aspects. Reading a book is very personal and the child has to tune his thoughts in tune with the author, by reading the entire book and understanding the message that the author seeks to convey. Watching a video gives a one-to-one interface with the author, as the graphics, music and pictures help in explaining the idea instantly. It is more personal and can be easily grasped by the child.
- The child can watch this video anywhere, any time and on any topic with low investment of money and time. This habit can be utilised when waiting at an airport, railway station, going on a long drive and even at a social gathering.
- Boosts mood when the child feels blue and low. It makes the child positive and can change *the entire focus of his life.*
- Keeps the child away from binge watching and mindless browsing.

Developing this Habit

- We can help the child make a choice, by gently persuading him to watch inspiring videos. We can suggest a few topics to guide them along, or better still watch a few videos with him. You can randomly ask questions, or better still, encouraging the child to be a critique and asking him to point out a couple of good things in the video. Don't be pushy; let them take their time. The child may not open up initially as he or she may be used to hearing you chide about this habit of 'mobile time'. Gradually during dinner time or when you feel that they are in the mood to chat, you can drop a hint about a good video and take it from there. Patience is the key and once this atmosphere of trust is built with the child he will let you into all the programmes that he watches. This habit of sharing opinions and content will help in a great way to reduce binge watching.

- One of the best ways is to make the child watch a minimum of three minutes of motivational video before watching anything else on mobile or internet. There are many self-development motivational speakers like Robin Sharma, Jack Canfield, Anthony Robinson, Virat Kohli, Arnold to name a few.

□

14

Habit of Time Audit

If someone asks what is the only thing that we have and yet may not have, it is Time! It means that time is the only valuable asset that one has. Time is limited and passes very fast. First, we kill time, than time kills us! In school, the child goes as per a timetable. This helps the child to learn management of time. Everyone has 24 four hours at their disposal, including the champion and the failure. The manner in which a child manages his 24 hours, decides his destiny. So, it becomes all the more important to teach the child habit of time-audit. The child has to be taught how to fit into his schedule a room for games and exercise, health and hygiene, learning and developing, recreation and family time. Not much attention is paid to this aspect in the school curriculum, as completion of syllabus is a priority and not time management.

Habit of Time Audit

It is a way by which a child is made to learn the value of time and account for the time he has. It is to teach how to use his time in an effective and systematic way.

Benefits of Time Audit

- Makes the child time-conscious. Time management benefits him in all areas of life.

- If he manages time well, he will have enough spare and leisure time to maintain a healthy work-life balance.
- Helps him avoid time stress. He can avoid stress and instead of trying to rush things, he can learn to fit things as per urgency and convenience.
- Makes him efficient and effective. The child becomes more organised. He can get more work done in a shorter period of time. It helps stay on the top of his tasks. It saves him from re-work, which often means starting the same task from zero.
- The child can learn to make priorities in life. It makes him more responsive and dependable.

Time Management

- The best way is to teach the child a habit called time-audit. Before sleep, the child may be asked to account for all the hours of the day spent, like from morning till night, what he has done fruitfully and, without wasting time.
- The other way is to teach the child to make a weekly tentative timetable. This should include all 168 hours of the week where he can jot down a tentative schedule to spend these 168 hours. It should include sleep, school-hours, games, hobbies, etc.
- As per research, the biggest obstacle in time management is multi-tasking. The child may be asked not to overlap one work over the other. If it is time for game, he must play the game and nothing else.
- Parents should teach children the value of time. The child should practice the habit of writing a diary wherein he can map or record his schedule. This will

help him realise the amount of time he devotes to a task and help him know where he is spending his major time.

- Child can use mobile app like Rescue time, Wunderlist, which help the child know where he spends his time.

□

15

Habit of Planning the Day

It is said that how you start your day is how you are going to live your day. And how you live your day is the way you live your life. The quality of your life depends upon the quality of your days! As per research, one minute of planning of the day saves 10 minutes of executing. One of the simplest yet highly rewarding habits to be imbibed in child is the habit of planning his day. It simply means that it is he who is 'running' the day, instead of day running him! The child will earn the maximum out of his day by following this simple habit. It is scheduling and prioritising his tasks for the day in such a way that it gives him maximum productivity and efficiency.

Planning the Day

It is giving priority to time as well as areas of life.

Benefits of Planning the Day

- It makes a child follow his tasks for the day automatically, without the pain of remembering them.
- Helps him prioritise the day and consequently his life.
- Keeps him focused on the areas/tasks which require his attention.
- Prevents him from deviating from his tasks/

goals. Even if he gets minimum of the tasks, he has scheduled, done, he is progressing.

- Gives him a schedule for the next day also in the form of incomplete tasks. It becomes a progress chart over a specified period like a month or a year.

Planning Your Day

- Before sleeping, the previous night or immediately after getting up in the morning, ask your child to make a checklist of the tasks, actions or goals he wants to do that day. Give a specific time slot and duration for each task. Write down the tasks very specifically. Give them ranking from 1 to 10 in priority. For example, you have seven tasks for one day. Choose the task which is most important and give it a specific time duration. Do not write ambiguous tasks like: I will exercise today (wrong method!). Rather write specific actions: I will exercise for 10 minutes after I have brushed my teeth at 8.30 a.m. (right approach).
- After the child has done this habit for 30 or more days, he can work out as to which time of the day is the most happening or productive time and which is his low time.
- Now, let him tick-off the completed tasks. It will give him a sense of accomplishment and help in getting positive feedback.
- Planning of the tasks should include all the major areas of life like health, school, sports, entertainment, hobbies, etc.

□

16

Habit of Saving

One of the most simple, helpful and rewarding habits for a child to learn is the habit of saving money. It is a common saying that we must save for our rainy days. A growing child generally does not have value for money as his thinking has not yet evolved as to how money is earned. The most common but innocent reply of a child if you ask him as to where from money comes, his reply is from ATM or bank! Developing the habit of financial prudence and saving should be one of the core purposes of parenting. The common rule is that at least 10 per cent of what the child gets, he should save.

Habit of Saving

Saving means paying yourself first. Generally a child gets regular pocket-money or some bucks for spending or for buying his stuff. Instead of expending all the money he has got, he is habituated to save some portion of it.

Benefits

- Helps to make the child value money and develop money-consciousness in him. Helps develop in him a lifelong attitude of saving. Helps in making him a better financial-planner.
- Helps the child make a better decision about finances. Instead of just spending what he gets, he consciously

chooses. This helps him make a better financial choice and develop the habit of better financial-decisions during his childhood. This becomes a full-fledged habit when he is an adult.

- Prods him to actually save a portion of what he gets which may seem meager but will turn up to be a handsome amount in the long run. His saving and interest on saving with compounding can give him a good financial start in his life.
- Small money saving habit can lead to many other habits of saving in life, like time-saving, resource saving, etc.

Developing the Habit of Saving

- Money saved is money earned and this habit of saving money can be taught by giving children pocket money and encouraging them to put a small portion of it in a piggy bank at home. When they grow slightly older say at teenage, parents may open a bank account for them. The money saved up in the piggy bank can then be counted in front of them, to create an impact. You can take your child to the bank and then open an account for him and transfer the saved money to his bank account.
- Whenever a child gets any money on his birthday or other social occasion or awards, prizes or gifts or earns from any activity, make him withhold a portion of it. Tell the child to put this portion in either a piggy bank or in his bank account. As a reward, parents can give an incentive of interest or an equal amount of money that the child has saved.
- Involve the child in chalking out the family-budget. Ask him for his suggestions on how to better use

financial resources. Ask him how the money can be saved.

- One of the simplest ways to teach the child the value of money is to give money as a reward for his activities once in a while. For example, send him to bring grocery or make him earn by selling waste newspapers which are piled up at home.
- Make the child collect all loose cash from various places at home and as an incentive, give a small portion to him for saving.

□

17

Habit of Choosing the Dress for Next Day in Advance

It is said that life is an occasion, so dress for it. The first thing we notice in others is their dress. Dressing sense speaks volumes about the traits of a child's personality. The best way to have a good dressing sense is to decide consciously the time, manner and occasion for the dress. For this a habit of pre-deciding the dress can be very helpful. Though it takes only 2 to 3 minutes, this habit can profoundly change the personality of a child.

Habit

It entails choosing and deciding the attire for the next day in advance. Before going to sleep, let the child collect all the items of his dress for the next day.

Benefits of Deciding on the Attire in Advance

- Improves the child's dress sense. A good selection of attire makes child look smarter, confident and more attractive.
- Gives the child sufficient time to choose and select his dress properly, wisely and appropriately. He can select his dress for the next day in a relaxed manner which is not the case in the morning on account of

pressing needs of morning schedule. Saves time and energy of the child in the morning.

- The child becomes more aware of his belongings in the cupboard. He becomes more organised in his day to day work routine. Also, this habit can encourage him to shop for his dress and other things on his own.
- Helps the child develop a habit of consciously 'choosing', instead of being swayed by the choices of others.

Making this a Habit

- Before going to bed, make the child select the dress for the next day and place it outside his wardrobe. Dress may include inner wear, pant and shirt, belt, wallet, socks, hanky, shoes and school bag. This dress selection may also include his dress post-school and sportswear. Well combed hair is part of good dress!
- Make the child try different combinations so as to bring more variety in his dress sense.
- Discuss with him the dress code suitable for a particular-occasion, like party, formal-occasion, casual wear. Give him a genuine compliment for his good dress. Ensure that the dress is neatly pressed and shoes cleaned and polished.
- Make him select his own dresses for family-holidays. Let him pack his stuff on his own.

□

18

Civic Habits

Children are the future citizens of a country. To encourage children to evolve into better human beings as well as better citizens, parents have the responsibility to teach them a few of basic civic habits. These small habits are a must for a healthy society and also for the health, wellbeing and safety of the children. The list of civic habits is long but I will limit these to a few basic ones only, viz.:

- (a) Habit of obeying traffic rules, (b) habit of wearing seat-belt, (c) habit of wearing a helmet.
- Habit of not littering public places.
- Treating everyone equally.

Benefits of Civic Habits

- Help the children to live safer, healthier and longer than those who are ignorant of these rules. They can protect themselves against accidents, disease and emergencies.
- Help them become a better citizen and member of society. It develops a feeling of responsibility in child.
- Develop a sense of belonging to the nation.
- Promote love and harmony among the fellow citizens, besides making them law-abiding citizens.

Traffic Habits

- In India one person dies every three minutes in road accidents. As per the data available, most injuries and deaths can be avoided if we follow the habit of wearing seat belts in automobile and helmets in two-wheelers.
- Sensitise your child against road accidents. Discuss the data and details with the child regarding deaths on account of road accidents and how to avoid these. Many videos are available on YouTube which show how wearing a helmet as well as a seatbelt has saved lives during accidents. Teach your child that it is not 'cool' to not wear a seat belt or helmet. Children must be encouraged to wear helmets even when they are cycling.
- Lead by example, for instance make it a point that whenever the family sits in car, everyone wears a seatbelt; even those who are sitting in the rear seats.
- The habit of obeying traffic rules is of utmost importance and must be imbibed from the beginning. Teach your child the basic rule's on how to cross roads and be vigilant while crossing roads or boarding and de-boarding the school bus.
- Sensitise the child about the dangers of over-speeding. Needless to say, while driving the personal vehicle, parents must adhere to speed limits so as to lead by example. This way, the child will learn to drive within the speed limit when he owns his own vehicle.
- One of the ways to teach the child is to take him once to a trauma-centre where victims of accident are being treated. This way he can see the pain and

agony suffered during an accident. This can register deeply in his mind.

Avoid Littering Public Places

- The basic value to teach the child is that our surroundings are an extension of our home. We cannot stay healthy if our own environment, be it public parks, roads, gardens and public-buildings are not clean.
- Start at home by teaching the child the habit of throwing the waste in dustbins. If he cannot find a dustbin in a public place, let him hold the waste and dispose it off at an appropriate place.
- Before going out, make sure he freshens himself up. This will help him restrict the use of public utility spaces. Teach him the value of public cleanliness against dangers of contracting malaria, dengue and other diseases.
- Always carry a small carry-bag while going out. Let the child put food-waste or wrappers of eatables in that bag instead of throwing in public-places.

Treating Everyone Equally

- Children are innocent souls. They do not make a distinction based on differences in caste, religion or class on their own. They learn these distinctions over time at home, school and society. Encourage your child to have diverse friendships and also expose him or her to various cultural experiences. Tell your child to find out what is best in other cultures.
- Never use any derogatory words for any other social group while discussing with the child or otherwise.
- One of the best ways to expose and sensitise the

child to the problems of others is role-play. For example, once in a while blind-fold the child and let him experience the difficulties faced by blind people. Then ask for his reaction and emotions. This exercise can be done to experience many of social problems and make him sensitive and compassionate to the pain and suffering of others and be empathetic to them.

□

19

Habit to Abstain from the Evils that Tempt the Youth

We live in an era wherein whatever is in vogue seems good and right. There are some evils in society which continue to plague our youth. Everyone knows the ill effects of these evil habits, but adopting them is seen as 'cool' these days. Our movies, songs and even role models seem to endorse these evils and end up confusing the vulnerable and impressionable minds. It is rare to find youth who do not give in to these evils. These habits develop during the early teenage years of a child who is still in his formative years. One of the purposes of parenting is to teach children the habit of abstaining from these evils.

Habit

Though there are many social evils, the most prevalent ones are—use of abusive language, violence, chewing of tobacco, smoking, drinking and using drugs.

Reason for Children Succumb to These Evils

- Curiosity for the unknown—pleasure/pain on consumption.
- To get relief from emotional distress or depression.

- The wish to appear adult and grown up and assert growing independence
- Peer pressure to fit in with friends.
- Family culture where parents, elder siblings indulge in them.
- To imitate actors or models who have appealing images in movies, video games or social media.

Develop Habit of Abstaining from These Evils

- Parents are the first role models for their children and they tend to imitate whatever they observe. Children do not listen or take direction but do what they like. You can be a role model for children by not indulging in these evils, be it smoking, drinking, tobacco, abusing under toxic effects or using drugs. Children, who live in the family which has a culture of any of these evils, are more likely to indulge in the habit as it triggers such behaviour and is considered normal in their system of values.
- Do not allow anyone to indulge in these evils and never send your children to buy or facilitate any of these items for you or for anyone else. Discuss the issue of these evils with your child when you see other people indulge. If there are adult smokers in the house, make sure they keep their cigarettes away from your child.
- Discuss with the child the immediate risks of these evils, like bad breath, less money in the pocket, hang-overs, bad temper, abusive language which are the results of this set of addictions. Emphasise on the ill effects and long-lasting risks that these evils have on their health and well-being and the likelihood of developing deadly diseases, less efficiency, wastage

of hard-earned money, deformed children, strained and unpleasant atmosphere at home, to name a few.

- One of the methods is to expose the child to the negative effects that these evils can cause. As per neuro-linguistic approach, if the child is exposed to these evils and their negative consequences, the child develops a repulsive feeling for these evils.
- Expose the child to those who have successfully quit these evils so that the child a holistic view of the situation.
- Expose the child gets to de-addiction centers. Let him feel the ills of these evils and realise how to come out of these evils.

□

20

Habits for Emergency-Preparedness

Life is full of twists and turns. There are occasions when a child may face a disaster, a trauma or an emergency-like situation. A few years back, there was a fire in a posh hotel in which many people lost their lives. Most of the survivors in this incident of fire were those who had been trained to save themselves from fire during their school days. To deal with such a situation, there are life-saving skills which a child must know to save himself and help others to survive. Emergency-like situations may be accidents, fire, medical emergency, electric shock, bomb blast, mob attack, theft, kidnapping attempt or assault, street fight, road rage or a natural disaster like an earthquake, case of drowning, lightning, flood etc.

Habit

It is best to prepare the child to save himself from an emergency.

Benefits of Emergency Preparedness

- Teaches the child the basic survival skills to live safe and sound.
- These skills can be used to rescue others.
- Fill the vital gap between the occurrence of the emergency and the arrival of help.

- Increases self-confidence of the child as he can face any emergency situation.
- Makes the child independent of his friends and peers in any emergency-situation.

Indication of These Skills

- Discuss with the child hypothetical situations of emergencies, like what would he do if suddenly there was an earth-quake? What would be his first reaction if there is a fire in the house? What he would do if someone tried to kidnap him? What would be the first number he would dial if any of his friends met with an accident? How would he come out of an accident damaged car? Simulate emergency situations like a heart-attack, accident, etc. and teach how to come out of it or save others.
- Teach him some basic life-saving skills like swimming, switch-off leaking cooking gas, give C.P.R., first-aid, etc.
- Make the child learn emergency numbers, like that of an ambulance, police, family doctor, fire-services.
- Let the child prepare a first-aid kit, emergency preparedness kit and medical kit.
- Make the child join life-saving training courses. These are easily available in many cities. There are videos available on internet which teaches the child life-saving skills. Make him join the National Service Scheme.

□

21

Habit of Reading

One of the simplest yet highly cogent habits is the habit of reading. If doing physical exercise is workout for the body, reading is a workout for the mind. We read either out of interest or for seeking answers. It is a must for every child. In the era of digital-world where the child is surrounded by gadgets and wizards, reading is imperative. During the formative years of the personality of child, whatever they learn through reading has a lasting impact.

Habit

It is the process that connects the mind of the child with the contents of a book.

Benefit of Reading

- Increases his word-power, memory and knowledge. It makes him smarter and better at understanding things. Reading improves his memory.
- Exposes the child to new ideas. It opens up his mind and gives him a new and different perspective on life. Reading helps him in changing his fixed-mindset to a growth-mindset.
- Helps in shaping his opinion and character. Reading makes him creative and imaginative. It helps the child to clarify the purpose of life. The habit of reading

helps the child obtain many answers to satisfy his inquisitive mind.

- Child can directly learn from the personalities who have attained success without having to try and test various methods himself. A book is basically an experience shared by the author about his journey to success.
- Develops into a lifelong hobby and habit. It saves the idle mind from any negative or futile thoughts and encourages positive thinking.
- Helps to know the tastes and interests of the child. Reading can also trigger him to be an author.

Making Reading a Habit

- Always keep a book on the bedside of the child. You should start by reading out a few paras to your child just before bedtime. The next step is to ask your child to read one para per day which may be extended to one page over time.
- Child observes parents more than anyone else and learns from them. Make reading a family value. Have a family reading hour every week. Tell the child to express his opinion on what he has learnt from the book. Discuss with him also what you have read.
- Initially, choose books covering a variety of topics, like fictional, adventure, mystery, fantasy, non-fiction, informative, general knowledge, scientific and even mythological books, so that the child may decipher where his interest lies.
- Make him read autobiographies of great personalities so that he can learn to be like them. Prompt him to read self-help books.
- Instal apps like Dropbox, Kindle or PDF Acrobat Reader in his phone. Start replacing his mindless

social media browsing with the habit of digital reading.

- Make the child carry a book whenever family travels for vacations. He can utilise his travel time and waiting-time at the railway-station or airport for reading.
- Let him find out various answers to question given in school and even learn from books instead from Google.

□

22

Habit of Learning a New Skill

As humans, we have multiple opportunities to learn new things and discover the hidden talents and potentials within ourselves. Very often we are either too lazy or procrastinate and let opportunities pass us by. A competitive attitude and desire to equip oneself with new skills should be encouraged in children. This will help them to discover their real potential. Every child is born with multiple talents. The talent of a child is varied and can be in singing, dancing, skating, sports, skiing, creative-writing, telling jokes or public speaking. The good part of parenting lies in understanding the potential of a child and encouraging and giving them exposure in the area that interests them.

Habit

It is learning other than the things a child knows.

Benefits of Learning a New Skill

- Makes the child unleash his hidden potential creativity and talent. By learning a variety of things, his learning speed increases.
- By learning and being exposed to a variety of skills, he is able to discover his true calling.
- Helps him to overcome boredom and monotony in life.

- Changes the brain chemistry of the child. As per research, it makes his brain more agile and helps in avoiding many physical and mental ailments, like dementia.
- Makes him more knowledgeable and better informed. It helps him in making connections between different skill areas.
- Makes him more interesting and helps him to win more friends as he has multiple talents and can jell well with other children with varied tastes.

Building this into a Habit

- List out all the tastes/inclinations a child is excited about. There is no limit to the human mind. The purpose of learning a new skill is not to be professional in that area; it is learning just for fun's sake. Expose him to different ideas, games, tastes and skills right from the beginning.
- Make him learn at least one new hobby every three months.
- If a child has an inclination to read, expose him to different genres of books like fictional, non-fictional, creative and imaginative books.
- If a child is good at physical activities, expose him to different games, yoga, dance, gymnastics and other skills associated with physical activities.
- If a child is good at music, expose him to classical singing, rapping, different musical forms, and may be even musical instruments. You never know how this new skill can come to the aid of a child in his later years of life.

□

23

Habit of Rating Your Day

As per a famous saying 'what gets measured, gets done'. In school, a child is rated for his progress in subjects on a scale of 1 to 100. The success and failure of the child is rated as average, good, very good or excellent, depending of the number or percentage of grades he gets. This is one of the time-tested ways to check his progress. Similarly, to get progress in all aspects of life, he needs to regularly assess his progress. Life is nothing but collection of days. So, one of the best ways to assess the progress of life is to develop the habit of measuring his progress on a daily basis.

Habit of Rating Your Day

Simply, it is making the child rate his each day on a scale of 1 to 10 with 10 being the maximum.

Benefits of Rating the Day

- Gives the child a basis to measure his progress on day-to-day basis.
- Keeps him self-accountable as he assesses his progress daily. Instead of parents forcing him to do something, he tends to do on his own. It helps him in overcoming bad or 'low days' and keeps him active and positive throughout the day.
- Keeps him focused and achievement-oriented.

It helps the child know what works for him and what does not. It makes him more creative as he always finds ways and means to improve on his achievements.

- Makes the child compete with himself than competing with others. He tries to outshine himself by himself. It gives him self-reflection feedback.

Making this a Habit

- Before going to bed, make the child rate his day on a scale of 1 to 10. The rating should cover various aspects of his daily life like health and fitness, school and career, family, finances, leisure and entertainment, personal goal, social goals, etc.
- Make him count even the smallest achievement to be included in rating. For example, taking a healthy diet, writing a poem, spending quality time with cousins and family, pursuing his hobbies, running 5 kms, helping an elderly person, finishing his homework in time, winning at sports competition, getting good grades, making a person smile, skipping junk-food etc.
- He can also rate his day as good, very good, excellent etc. However, rating on a measurable scale is more specific, accurate and rewarding. The rating should be done against specific and measurable acts done during the day. The overall rating of 5 plus indicates that he is progressing. His rating of the day would ultimately decide his rating in different areas and in life.

□

24

Habit of Developing a Good Handwriting

A good handwriting often defines one's personality. As per graphology (art of reading handwriting), it is not the hand which writes; it is the brain which writes through our hands! The first impression that a child makes at school is through his handwriting. So much so, a few years back, a good handwriting would secure a bonus of 5 to 10 marks, as an encouragement to children to develop a good handwriting. Cursive writing books were part of the pre-primary syllabus and competitions are held even today, in calligraphy, to hone the skill in good handwriting. Parents should make sure their kids learn the skill of a legible and neat handwriting knowing very well the value placed on it in the examinations. I have come across many students preparing for competitive exams and putting in special effort to improve their handwriting so as to score more in written exams.

Habit

The habit of good handwriting is to write in a neat, clean and legible manner.

Benefits

- In examinations where written tests are one of the main criteria for judging a child, a good handwriting plays a vital role in scoring good marks. A pleasing handwriting is a pleasure for any teacher to correct.

- Even if a child is good at learning things mentally, until and unless he cannot pen them down in a legible and neat handwriting, he would be in a disadvantageous position in comparison to his peers.
- It is a life-long skill which helps him using this skill on many visual communications like hand-written letters or greeting cards, or any other form of written medium.

Developing the Habit of Good Handwriting

- One of the easiest ways is to tell the child to write an essay, or an article in 200 words on any topic of his choice. If he likes playing video-games, tell him to write about it. The next day make him point out his own flaws in terms of his handwriting, like spacing, neatness, clarity, jotting the words within the ruled lines, maintaining equal gaps between alphabets and words in a sentence. Tell the child to grade his own writing on a scale of 1-10, 10. Now, you can do grading on a scale of 1 to 10 so that the child can understand his flaws and not repeat them. Very gently but firmly ask him to repeat the process until the end result is pleasing to the eye. Although it is hard work on the part of a parent, gentle coaxing and encouragement will bring out the best in your child.
- Encourage children to draw and develop good strokes and neatness at an early age. A good handwriting is a skill as well as an art. So make practicing this art a habit of fun.
- Make him write on greeting cards or invitation cards to hone his skill in good handwriting.

□

25

Habit of Tuition

There are two purposes of education: (a) teach the child how to learn, (b) teach him how to live life. Ironically, there is a cut-throat competition for marks, grades, percentage among the children and more so among the parents. The purpose of modern education has become to get high scores which have overshadowed the real purposes of education i.e. learning. We are less bothered as how much the child understands a subject but are more concerned about how many marks he gets in that subject. In this era of race for marks, parents are resorting to tuition for their child. Earlier only the weaker students were given tuition but now-a-days tuition-classes have become just an extension of schools! And on many days, the child spends more time in tuition-class than in school! The habit of tuition is neither out rightly bad nor inherently good. It depends upon many factors, like the level of child's learning, the efforts of school teachers, the role of parents, their financial capacity, the level of competition, etc.

Reasons for Attending Tuition

- Child does not understand teaching at school.
- Teachers do not teach well in school.
- To pass examinations or to get higher marks/good score in examinations.

- Parents' decision.
- Because friends and classmates also go for tuition.

Habit of Tuition

It is getting teaching in small groups besides school teaching.

Benefits of Tuition

- Every child has an individual and unique learning experience. It helps the one-on-one attention of teacher and student which is mostly missing in schools because of high teacher-student ratio.
- Improves academic performance of the child and helps improve his attitude towards learning.
- Improves self-esteem and confidence of the child besides improving his work and study habits.
- Helps him understand and learn better as there is repetition of the syllabus.

Disadvantages

- Child spends too much time on tuitions. He starts finding study to be a burden and the monotony and boredom of tuitions makes him lose interest in studies. The only thing a child learns in tuition is academics and not anything else, like in school where there are co-curricular activities and other forms of learning. So, it is just a competition for more facts and numbers.
- Erodes his attention and interest in classroom as that child thinks that he is going to get this learning anyway in tuition. He becomes complacent.
- Tuition eats up other areas of his life like sports, recreation and games.

- It also adds to financial burden on the pocket of the parents.

Decision on Taking Tuition

- The extra tuition has become a trend. It is like getting the same stuff at tuition by paying more than what the child is offered at school! So, tuition should be just subject-specific tuition and not a must for all the subjects.
- The best antidote for tuition is the habit of self-study. The child enjoys his study and it also sparks an interest in studies. Parents must strive to make self-study the core habit of the child.
- Another way is for parents to spend at least 45 minutes per day to teach the child themselves. This way they will understand the needs of the child more than the tutor.
- The best way to learn is learning by fun. Parents should try integrating his syllabus with practical things, like show him historical movies, education and knowledge channels like Discovery, History Channel, etc. Download for him various educational games, like Spelling Game, Learning Maths Game, etc.

□

26

Habits for Success in Exams

Every child has to clear exams which are held in every school, irrespective of the pattern or Board the school follows. The purpose of taking exams at regular intervals is to test the level of their learning and understanding. They are seen as the test of their learning. The learning levels of our children are tested by exams such as language-skills, aptitude, critical-thinking, general knowledge, or specialised subjects. Both our education system as well as classroom teaching is largely exam-oriented. The purpose of classroom teaching has become to prepare the child for the coming exams and clear the exams with good marks. Children are taught in the classroom from an examination point of view. We may dislike the present examination system but it is unavoidable reality of our education system and followed even in the professional and non-professional courses and competitive exams. By the time a child finishes his 12th standard, he has already appeared in more than 72 exams! For a child, exams are a 'monster'! Many a time a child does not perform good in these exams, not because he did not have the learning, but because he did not have the required skills and habits for getting success in exams. The following are few of the habits which will help the child to face the exams and 'crack' them with good grades.

Habit

Habit for success in exams is an art and skill which helps the child to get good grades, scores, marks or percentage. It has three components: (a) how to prepare for exams, (b) skills for the exams day (c) how to effectively write exams.

Reasons for Under-performance in Exams

The following reasons could be an eye opener for parents when their child under performs:

- The child might not actually have followed his syllabus prescribed for the exams.
- Fear of exams or examination phobia which affects the child.
- The child may be under pressure to outperform his peers, or may be under pressure from parents to score high marks and grades. He may be a victim of the marks-race in which marks are the criteria of intelligence.
- Too many of tests and exams create tension in the child. Testing the knowledge of the child in just three hours has many variable factors.
- The examiner can only evaluate and base his judgement of the knowledge of the child as per the syllabus and the written output that is presented in a specified time.
- Bad handwriting.
- The child may not know the art, skill and effective habits essential in writing exams.

Developing Habits for Success in Exams

- Since, the whole test of learning and grading a child depends upon the way the student attempts the exams, it is necessary to develop good writing skills in the child. The first impression on the examiner is handwriting. Until and unless the child has an impressive handwriting, the chances of scoring good marks are low. This is true in higher classes as well as in competitive exams that have subjective and descriptive types of questions. For example, the second stage of IAS. exams is completely descriptive and narrative.

- There are cut-throat competition and high expectations of parents for high marks. This gives rise to guilt in the child if he under performs. This pressure can lead to many bad tendencies in the child. Parents must encourage the child to perform well but not pressurise. The role of a parent is to create a positive environment and help the child cope with competitions and exams.
- The best way is to have simulated exams and tests at home in a stress-free and relaxed environment. Ask the child to be an examiner and check his own test and give marks as he deems fit. Ask him to underline the mistakes and jot down the comments. Encourage him to give marks for handwriting, completion of paper, length of the answer and correctness of the answer.
- Most children write what they know, instead of what is asked in the question. Teach the child to first read the question three times and understand what the question is asking and what it is not asking. Examiner wants to know if the child knows what he is asked to know. Teach him to mentally write the answer which will take hardly 10 seconds before he puts it in writing. Time management and completion of all answers is the key for a child to score high marks.
- Tell the child how to write a test not only during exam-days but also as part of a weekly routine. Make him mentally solve the answers and let this be his favourite pastime and fun.
- The child should get a sound sleep a night before. He should take a light meal before the exams. He should go with a feeling that it is just a test of his learning and not life.

□

27

Selecting Friends

It is said that man is the average of five persons he spends the most time with. Nothing can be truer about this saying with respect to children. So much so, the child is identified with the peers and friends he hangs out with; in short, the company he keeps. In teen years, children tend to spend more time with friends than with their parents. The most important ideas, influences and impressions are shaped by his peers and friends. Peer pressure can be both positive and negative. One of the most important but also difficult tasks for parents is to teach the child as to whom he should befriend.

Value

It is how the child selects as to who would be his friend.

Importance of Company

- It is only in company that the child develops as a social being.
- There are numerous empirical evidences which suggest that the actions, opinions, ideas, habits and character of the child is shaped and determined by the company of his friends.
- Good friends give him fond memories for life, while bad ones teach him lessons for life.

- Most role-models of a child are influenced by his friends.

Selection of Friends

- Children normally make friends based on certain qualities that they appreciate in another. It is better to allow the child to choose and make his own friends. As parents, you can guide and instruct the child on what qualities to look for, like being selfless and not harmful to them as an individual. You can listen, observe and then discuss your child's friends only if the child opens up to you. Do not be judgmental.
- It is important to teach the child the negative aspects of peer pressure resistance. Children are more likely to fall into the trap of smoking, alcohol or drugs offered by friends.
- A child observes whatever we do. They may decide on their friends on the basis of how we make and treat our friends. Be a good and honest friend so that most likely your child will carry forward this feeling, whilst he makes his friends. Teach your friend what it is to be a good friend, so that he too can imitate you and be a good friend to his friends.
- Do not be a party to a dispute of your child with his friends. Just listen, but let the child handle the fight.
- Make your home a child-friendly home where the child and his friends like to come. This way we can see what influences the children are having and we, as parents, can guide them accordingly.
- Don't worry about whether your child has the right number of friends. Some prefer just one best friend; while others like to be part of a large group of friends.

□

28

Value for Healthy Sibling Relationship

Siblings are children from the same parents while cousins are children of an uncle or aunt. In a single family, the child interacts with his siblings only, while in joint families, he deals with both siblings as well as cousins. This relationship between siblings is one of the most important relationships which influence the mental, emotional and psychological make-up of the child. There is competition and sharing for physical things, like clothes, toys, T.V. remotes, gifts and other things; for emotional things, like the attention of parents, relatives and friends; for psychological needs like the desire to outdo the other, arguing, dominance etc. After friends, the maximum time a child spends is his with siblings. Siblings can be the best friend or the worst rival. So, healthy sibling relationship is an important aspect in the healthy grooming of a child. The purpose of developing this habit is to teach the child to grow himself by growing his siblings/cousins.

Value

Sibling relationship is how a child deals with his brother or sister and the nature of the relationship is integral in the making of their personalities.

Benefits of Healthy Sibling Relationship

- This relationship between siblings is the longest

relationship in a child's life. This relationship prepares the child on how to deal with the world.

- Makes the child more selfless as he shares his things, belongings and emotions.
- Gives the child an emotional bond which can give him a support and recluse.
- Healthy competition between the siblings can make the child active, physically fit, agile and adjusting.

Developing a Healthy Sibling Relationship

- Ask what the good qualities which the others have are. Also ask what are the qualities which one child does not have and which he would like to imbibe from the other. Also ask for the things which they do not like about each other. The purpose of this exercise is to teach them that each child is unique and has some good qualities as well as weaknesses.
- Once in a week, ask the children to tell what acts and things they like about each other in that week.
- The other important exercise is to ask the child to share and gift his favourite belonging, like a book, game or dress to the other. This will impart the feeling of sharing.
- If there is a fight between them, do not interfere or take a side. Let them negotiate for a win-win situation.
- Keep aside a special family hour, preferably a family dinner, once in a week. Let everything be discussed over the dinner table.

□

29

Respect the Opposite Sex

This is one of the values which must be imbibed strongly in the child, especially a boy-child. Without this value, all other values are incomplete. It is respect for the woman. She is the creator whom God has entrusted with the responsibility of giving birth. In every culture of the world, anything which gives birth is hailed as mother; like mother-land, Mother-Earth, etc. Teach the child to respect women from the very beginning. Respect has three aspects. Respect by words means 'listen' to them, respecting and accepting their opinions and, respecting them as equal. It means being polite to them by saying please and thank you. It also means not saying harsh words like 'shut up' or 'get lost' to them. Respect by actions: Teach the child about touching, teasing or staring at women. Also, teach them not to ever hit or threaten girls or women. Respect by thoughts also means not treating them as objects.

Value

Respect every woman for being a woman and an equal member of the society.

Why This Habit

- It is a basic human value. Woman represents other half of the family and society. God has created everyone equally.
- It teaches the child the value of respect and to be kind.

- Girls have some natural qualities, like care and innocence. By respecting these values, the child may imbibe these values.

Teaching the Value of Respect for a Girl

- The mothers have a crucial role in making this habit. The way a child sees his mother as how she treats herself, how she treats other women and how and what she talks about other women and girls makes a huge impact on the child.
- Further, the way a boy child sees his father and other males of family treating their mothers, wives and daughters will cast a great impression on how a boy treats a girl. If the men in their lives think it is right to stare and whistle at women, or tease them, or think them to be weak, or abuse women and call them names, then the chances of him picking up these impressions are high.
- You can ask your child these questions: If you are a father, how will you make your sons respect women? If you are a mother, how will you make your sons respect women?
- Imbibe the value of respect by being an example. Respect of woman starts with respect of the mother. As parents, we need to respect our children, our parents, elders, other adults, and especially respect women.
- When you find your boys criticising women because of their logic or driving ability, or for any other gender-related issue, pull them up for it. Let them know sexism is neither cool nor funny.
- Limit their exposure to violent media and such contents in which a woman is objectified. Teach the child the harmful effects of watching pornography.

□

30

Respecting Parents and Thanking Them

There is a visible change in the behaviour of current generation towards their parents. We hear of many incidents of children disrespecting, bullying and even abusing their parents. At the core of this disrespect lie two prevalent perceptions: (a) feeling of entitlement which makes the children think that they are entitled to all what their parents are giving, be it unconditional love or privileged upbringing; (b) disrespect from children who fail to appreciate the efforts made on their behalf by their parents. This value of 'respecting parents' is eroding and weakening due to laxity amongst parents, as the family size has shrunk to a single child or two children. Parents these days dote on their children, give in to their demands, spoil them by buying expensive gifts and then complain or feel frustrated when the child disobeys or deceives them!

One of the most basic values a child should develop is thanking, respecting, caring and loving his parents. We are in the world because of our parents. Many of our ideas, values and good things are fathered by our parents. The child must be groomed in such an environment that he should always and forever respect his parents. Parental love for children is the purest, unending and selfless love. If a child cannot develop love for his parents, it is difficult to imagine he can love anyone else. There are countless things our parents do for us and we will never be able to pay back for their favours. That is why many religions equate parents with God.

Value

Children should be taught to develop this value of respecting and loving their parents, grandparents and elders.

Reason for Disrespecting Parents

- If parents are disrespectful themselves, be it to their child or their own parents or others.
- If parents ignore the emotional needs of their child.
- Not accepting the child for who he is or imposing their own choices to fit their vision of who he should be by the parents
- Lack of family values regarding unconditional love and acceptance on the part of parents.
- If parents are not honest, upright and forthright.
- A generation gap

Developing Love and Respect for Parents

- Let the child do small acts for parents, like cook a meal for them, go to the temple with them, join a common hobby with them, like swimming, dancing, cycling, etc.
- Ask the child to spend quality time with parents and know about their life experiences. The most valuable thing a child can offer his parents is his time.
- Parents should be their role models. If the parents respect their parents, i.e. the child's grandparents, automatically the child will respect you. Also, whenever possible, make the child spend more time with cousins, grandparents and extended family.

This will help in developing family bond of love and affection.

- Let parents be the world's best friends. Spending quality time with children, like helping them with their work, knowing more about their school life, friends, day-to-day experiences at school/workplace will only be shared if parents develop a rapport with their wards.
- Teach the child to say one specific sentence of thanking his parents daily, like 'I am thankful you have given me good schooling', 'I am thankful you have given me good food', 'I am thankful you have given me love and care' so and so forth.
- One of the biggest mistakes that parents are guilty of and which they commit is by substituting 'child time' with expensive gifts. It should never be the case.
- Keep aside a family hour. Have at least one family meals together in a week.
- Let the child share his feelings with you unconditionally. Even if the child is a rebellious child, give him enough space to express himself.

□

31

Habit of Being Kind to Nature

There are only two abodes which a human being inhabits: his body and planet Earth. Both these abodes are important for our survival and sustenance. The child, who is the future of this planet, must imbibe the value of being one with nature. The best way to enhance the life of planet is to teach the child to nurture it. This idea of 'one with nature' is imparted in the Japanese education system. In Finland, there is the concept of 'forest school' where children can spend up to 95 per cent of the school day outdoors, exploring, playing and learning hands on. The child is allowed to dirty himself in the sand, drink from streams, pluck fruit from trees and listen to the chirping of birds in the world around him. With the rising levels of pollution and ecological imbalance, many a school has included tree plantation drives in the school curriculum through project work.

Being Kind to Nature

It makes the child understand that humans and nature are co-existent and cannot survive without the other. The best way to nurture the earth is to plant trees. Another way is to conserve our resources and not overuse or waste land, water or air.

Benefits of Being Kind to Nature

- Gives him a lifelong hobby and interest. It makes the child happy, contented and accomplished.

- Spends more time away from digital clutter.
- Keeps him healthy, fit and agile. A recent research shows that who spend time with nature live much longer, and are less prone to disease and illness. Even doctors in Europe have started recommending nature walks.
- Nature has its own healing, spiritual and mystic powers which can help the child live in harmony in the environs.
- It grooms him in becoming a responsible citizen.

Developing this Value

- The best method to develop this habit is to make the child plant trees. It will make him value nature as well as acquire hands-on experience in planting a tree or a sapling. Make tree plantation a family affair. When the whole family engages in plantation of trees, this habit develops automatically in the sub-conscious mind of the child. Plantation on special occasions, like the birthday of a grandparent, gifting a tree sapling on festive occasions will encourage the child to be kinder and one with nature.
- Make gardening a hobby and the best way to imbibe interest of the child in this is by encouraging the child to learn gardening. This, apart from being a recreational activity, can create in him a love for plants and nature. Start a vegetable garden at home and this will prompt the child to participate in it.
- Teach the value of minimalism. The best way to preserve nature is to use minimum resources, be it water, air or land. We have to teach them that our mother planet does not only belong to them but their future generations also.
- The child should be made aware about the rising

levels of pollution and also sensitised to the methods for controlling pollution. The three R's of sustainability are reduce, reuse and recycle, Make sure that you have a recycling bin at home and teach the child to recycle water and other items.

- Teach the value of compassion towards birds and animals. Co-existence of human beings with other creatures of the planet is one value which can go a long way in making them one with nature. One way to spark their interest is to make them watch the series, **Man vs Wild** and other channels like **Discovery, Animal Kingdom and National Geographic**.

□

32

Habit of Gratitude

We, as well as our children, take life for granted. We have many material things like good-food, dresses, a nice home, a good car or intangible things like good, health, schooling, family, a good hobby, etc. Once a child was unhappy with a pair of shoes he wore and was cribbing. Suddenly, he saw a poor child who had no legs! He was stunned and realised how much he had. Gratitude is the habit of being thankful for all the abundance and prosperity that a child has in life and celebrates it. Gratitude is being thankful, sometimes, for absence of pain or sorrow also! Gratitude is one habit which can really change the outlook of the child towards life. We should cultivate 'the habit of gratitude' consciously so as he does it daily.

Habit

Make the child thankful for what he has, be it material or spiritual.

Benefits of the Habit of Gratitude

- Gives a positive start to the day and sets in a good mood of the child.
- Makes the child focus on what he has in life and be aware of the abundance and prosperity he has.
- Gives more power to the child to handle a bad mood,

ups and downs, emotional outbursts and even a negative situation.

- Best antidote to the common habit of cribbing. It makes the child happier and optimistic.
- Withdraws the mind from what a child does not have and removes negative thinking.
- Triggers positive thoughts, especially when he sees the less fortunate around him.
- Makes the child friendlier and social as when he expresses gratitude to someone, the other person appreciates him.

Developing the Habit of Gratitude

- Ask the child to make five specific affirmations in the morning before he gets out of the bed. These affirmations can be like, 'I am thankful to God as I am awake and alive', 'I am healthy and fit', 'I have caring parents', 'I have loving siblings and relatives', 'I have a good family', 'I have a good school and good friends', 'I am going to have a good day which will be much better than any other day', 'I have good clothes, toys, games, T.V.' etc.
- Teach him to make a list of all things and blessings he has like a new gift, a new friend, a good holiday, etc. and also list out what other children do not have.
- Imbibe in the child the value to compare his life with others who are less fortunate in material possession but when it comes to growth and success, he should compare with those who are ahead of him in terms of success.
- The first person we have to thank is God for the wonderful life he has blessed us with. We can also be thankful for the wealth and opulence that he has blessed us and our family with, be it a good school

that you go to, or the wonderful classmates, teachers and friends that we have in your life.

- We can go a step further and be indebted that our parents have a good job, and are able to give financial security which would prove beneficial in fulfilling our ambitions and dreams. We should be enthusiastic about the time we spend with our grandparents, who shower their unconditional love on us. Most importantly, we must appreciate our mother who works tirelessly and makes you comfortable at home and in life.

□

33

De-clutter Your Mind

De-clutter simply means remove the unnecessary! Our mind is the sum total of our thoughts, images and ideas we have stored within. De-cluttering the mind simply means removing unnecessary ideas, information, thoughts, persons, events, incidents, etc. from the mind. How to de-clutter the mind? There are two ways of doing this. One is to focus on something positive or higher than the current state of thoughts. Like living the idea of higher goals, aims, and pursuits, for example a young child with a dream to become a cricketer absorbs his mind only on the thought of being a successful cricketer or through meditation where we focus on our inner-self on subconscious mind. The second way is removing a specific person, thought, information or event from the memory.

Habit

De-clutter of mind means removing something from the mind or absorbing the mind in a chosen flow of thoughts.

Benefits of De-cluttering the Mind

- Releases negative energy. He can use this extra energy for a good purpose which makes him positive.
- Simplifies a child's life. He becomes stress-free and can focus on the core areas of his life.
- Gives peace of mind and calmness to child.

- Helps the child connect to himself where he can have a positive self-talk with himself.

De-cluttering the Mind

- Try forgiving at least one small bad experience in life on a daily basis. For example, someone had spoken ill-words about you three years ago, the mind still holds the grudge whenever the child comes across that person. One fine day, you consciously decide to forgive that person in your mind. This leads to slowly forgetting that person and the event.
- Try forgetting specific unpleasant past events. For example, someone played with you emotionally. Forget that person and remove him or her from your contacts or memory timeline. This gradually removes that person from your memory. Sometimes forgetting leads to forgiving.
- Try to take some bad incidents in life as destiny or destined. Simply accept some things in life as they are.
- Get a load off by sharing with others. If you have an emotional bond, or a trust worthy person (difficult to find these days!), try to unburden your thoughts with him or her.
- There are a few small steps which can de-clutter the child's mind. Reduce watching television! Go off social media at least two hours a day. Reduce intake of unnecessary information like news on violence, etc.
- Try blocking the persons who send you frivolous messages or forward messages on WhatsApp or other social media. Go through your phone contact book. The contacts, to which you have not contacted for the last one year, can be deleted.

□

34

Habit of Decision Making

One of the core habits of parenting is to teach the child the habit of decision-making. What we are today is the sum total of our choices and decisions. What makes a successful person different from an unsuccessful person is the kind and nature of choices the former makes. Even if, we do not make a choice that is also a choice! So as a human being we always have the choice to choose. The process of selecting among the available choices is known as decision-making ability. This habit of decision making is not a one-time affair or event, but an ongoing process which one keeps on practicing.

Habit

It is choosing the best out of the available choices and may be any small like choosing his dress or major choice as his career.

Benefits of Decision Making

- Makes the child more responsible. If a choice is made by him, he would not react or crib or blame others for the results that may ensue.
- Helps the child play an active role in life. Instead of being swayed by the decisions of his peers, he chooses to assert his choice. New-found confidence due to right decision making prevents him from succumbing

to peer-pressure or being dominated by others.

- This habit is the best recipe against laziness or procrastination because by making a choice, he takes the first step towards action.
- Develops the mental and intellectual capacity since the child has to choose from several options.
- Takes into account the circumstances before coming to a particular decision. It strengthens his learning abilities as he has to develop the habit of coming up with innovative ideas.
- Develops into an informed, confident and independent social being, as he gradually masters the habit of decision making.
- It helps the child to identify his own strengths and weaknesses. This awareness equips the child to be in an advantageous position when faced with challenges and problems.

How to Developing the Habit of Decision Making

- Let the child express preference or choice on smallest of the smallest of issues. Give him preferences and let him make a choice. For example, let him chose his dress or his items of daily use or the colour of brush or a particular brand of soap.
- Teach him to take a few seconds and think before leaping. It will help him to see multiple options. Get your child to ask questions and evaluate the options. Let him understand why he wants to do this and what are his options.
- Involve him in family decision-making processes, be it the family-budget, destination for holidays, choice school, sports, career, etc. One of the best exercises is to give the child simulated or hypothetical situations so that he makes choices or decisions at least on

the mental level. Like, if he is a father how would he spend times with children, how would he be setting family-budget etc.

- Give money and a grocery list and watch from a distance how he purchases the items. Observe if he checks the prices of various commodities on sale. You may assist him at the billing counter in a very positive manner, without hurting his sentiments in case he exceeds the budget. This practical lesson helps him to prioritise and make a sensible selection.

□

35

Habit of Creativity

Creativity means to think 'out of box', to adopt an unusual approach, to invent or display original ideas. As per research, every human being is creative and creativity is inherent and is the most important characteristic of being human. Research says each human being is creative by birth! A child displays this trait of creativity when he or she imagines or fantasises before being schooled. Such is the power of imagination that he can use his imagination to assume his pillow as a toy, or as an aero plane, a ship or even as horse on which he rides! There is no limitation to his creativity. Slowly, he enters the school system, where he is taught' to fit in. He is taught not to think differently but according to what the society wants of him! Our present education system typically undermines the daydreams, imagination or imperfection—all those attributes that great minds said were keys to their revolutionary ideas. The child's creative ability is replaced by following the prescribed syllabus that curbs his other cognitive aspects. The ultimate purpose of education and parenting is to bring out what is unique and creative in your child.

Habit of Creativity

It is making the child think 'out of box' or think differently by using his own powerful imagination or thoughts.

Benefits of Creativity

- Promotes thinking and helps in teaching problem-solving.
- Makes the child free from monotonous thinking and trying out ideas while rendering him or her stress free.
- Renders him 'free' from what the society teaches out. Creativity makes the child to be innovative.
- On accessing his thoughts and ideas to solve anything, he discovers his own strengths and weakness.
- All great personalities of the world were creative, like Newton, Einstein, Zuckerberg to name a few among the trailblazers.

Promoting the Habit of Creativity in Children

- Let the child think independently without any prompting or guidance by the parents on some specific issues. Ask your child to come up with alternative solutions.
- Allow the child to be exposed to radical and opposite ideas. For example, if people think that we should make skyscrapers above the earth, make your child debate on the concept of alternative possibilities like making skyscrapers underground.
- Do not snub the child when he comes with any unusual ideas or thoughts. Do not tell that the answer is wrong as it does not conform to what is written in books, try to ignite his thought process by giving him more time to answer.
- Expose the child to different creative exercises. Create an atmosphere for creative tasks and activities at home, like writing a story or drawing or sketching.
- Encourage the child to read books that relate to fantasy with imaginative creatures, which have

unusual names and live otherworldly lives, different from normal human existence.

- Let the child be exposed to ideas and places that can help him have alternate answers. Take him to a library, museum, an animal safari or even a different state in the country.
- Teach him that the purpose of education is not cramming or scoring good marks but to bring creativity out of him to make him understand the world around them.
- Make him read books on creativity, like *The Agile Mind- How Your Brain Makes Creativity Happen,* etc.

□

36

Habit of Acknowledging One's Achievements

One of the simplest yet powerful habits is the habit of acknowledging our achievements. Whenever we resolve to improve upon ourselves, a thought flashes across our mind—have we wasted, our precious time and life? It is but natural to think so, when we feel that as per the world's standards, we have fallen short of expectations. This is factually not true as we are all unique individuals. We must appreciate our each past achievement and keep reminding ourselves of the good things that have taken place in our lives. Every child has done and achieved something or the other in some field or the other—be it emotional, physical or tangible and related to areas of finances, family, professional, personal, health or fitness. It can really change the child's mindset from having no achievement in life to a life which is full of action and wonderful achievements! We must teach the child to inculcate the habit of focusing on his achievements and appreciating them.

Habit

It is making the child acknowledge, admit and appreciate all the positive things he has done in life.

Benefits of Acknowledging Past Achievements

- The child acknowledges his past in a positive way. It makes him positive. He realises that his life has not been worthless but is full of positive successes, however small they may be. It removes his regret at not doing any worthwhile thing in life.
- It inspires the child to achieve more in life as he is confident that he has already achieved many things in life.
- It gives him a sense of belief that he did better than many who did not even try. It will make him action-oriented as also achievement-oriented.
- It makes the child compete with himself in terms of achievements instead of competing with others.
- Acknowledging the past inspire the child to value his past. This positive inspiration helps him in being positive in life.

How to Develop this Habit?

- Make the child draw a list of all the positive actions he has taken in his life however small they may seem to be like winning a quiz competition, getting selected as a team member of school table-tennis team, being head-boy or girl, being member of a school committee, performing a dance in society-building, winning an open debate competition, completing a tough track, being praised by the teachers, helping a needy, sharing something with classmate, etc. These above examples are very small actions but still they are achievements. The golden rule is to remember that it is his life and his achievements and if he does not feel good about his actions, then who will?

- Every day before going to bed, make the child think of one positive action that he has done during the course of the day. He may think not only about the successful action but even the effort put in to take an action, irrespective of the outcome of the action. For example, the child may have tried to save an injured bird, though the bird might not have survived.

□

37

Habit of Improvement

Improvement is a basic pre-condition for growth. What a child is today is the result of his habits. His present habits have brought him where he is. But to progress and grow in life, habits need to grow and improve. One of the best habits to imbibe in the child is to improve upon whatever he does. Success is a slow incremental daily progress culminating in unimaginable results. While goals give the child direction, habit of improvement gives him the path and progress. It is micro progress which compounds to stunning achievements later. If a child improves his habit by one per cent per day, it can lead to 37 times improvements in that particular field in a year!

Habit of Improvement

The habit of improvement signifies adding more to whatever positive a child does in terms of quantity and quality. Suppose child does 10 push-ups a day, habit of 1% improvement means doing 11 push-ups and adding different versions of push-ups.

Benefit of Habit Improvement

- Habit of one per cent improvement may seem insignificant but the compound benefits are immense and multiple.

- Even a slight improvement makes and sustains a habit which trickles down to all spheres of life and excellence becomes a life philosophy of the child.
- Saves the child from boredom of making and developing a good habit.
- Gives variety and develops creativity in life as the child is always looking for different ways of improvement.
- It works against complacency in any sphere of life.

Developing the Habit of Improvement

- Identify the good habits in the child. Start working on these habits. Ask the child as to how he can do better and improve his habits. It is progress in any field, however small it may be. If the child has a habit of eating a fruit, improvement may not mean eating two fruits, but tasting different fruits. If he takes a banana, improvement may be in taking another fruit like an orange or a pear or bowl of mixed fruits. If he exercises for 30 minutes, it may mean not only more time for exercise but more vigorous and variety in exercise.
- Tell him to identify the areas and spheres where he can make just 1 % improvement be it how he dresses, how he studies, how he attempts his exams, how he eats meals etc.
- Make him do more of the action in terms of quantity and quality. If he reads one page per day, make him read one extra para with more focus and intensity.
- If he has a bad habit, change it by stacking a good habit. If he takes three cold drinks in a day, advise him to take a glass of juice before he takes his cold drink.

□

38

Finding Passion

Human beings are emotional beings. When emotions become intense for a reason, they are known as a passion. Every child is born with an inborn passion. A child may have many interests and tastes like sports, painting, dancing, driving, fashion, acting, reading, to name a few. When the child is forced to follow his parents' ambition or dream, it usually ends in producing an average result. Nothing great has been achieved in this world without passion. Without the child finding his passion, he will remain average in whatever he does. Passion may be an activity, hobby or an idea that gives goose bumps to the child and sparks him. He can spend his uninterrupted time, energy and focus following his passion, pursues it till he has achieved success in it. So, the very purpose of parenting is discovering the passion of the child!

Value

It is finding the real kick or what makes the child move and sets him on fire without being forced by anyone.

Benefits of Identifying the Passion of Child

- Gives a definite direction, purpose and kick to the child. Passion helps in realising the true and full potential of the child. His own passion will be the driving force in his life and not idle threats or punishments to do something of his parents' liking as that eventually leads to unfulfilled dreams.

- Helps the child to narrow-down a profession or career, which he can adopt integrating his passion with the profession.
- Helps the child to focus on his core strength rather than working on dreams of others.

Locate Passion in Your Child

- You should start asking questions. Is there something a child already loves doing? Does he excel in that area? Does the child spend endless hours on that particular activity? Is there an activity in which the child finds himself in the flow? Do you encourage your child in the area that interests him? Do you force your child to give up his passion, for something more lucrative that he can turn into a profession? These questions can give you a fair idea to zero in on the probable passions of the child.
- There are many a things a child loves doing. Parents can find their child's passion out of these activities and then focus on one. It may be a game, literary item, dance, computer games etc.
- One of the ways to find out the passion of the child is to find where he spends his time in reading? What does the child spend hours on reading about or browsing about?
- Introspection is yet another way to discover the passion of the child. Parents must ask, ask and ask the children as to what their true calling is or what kicks them. They must discuss the career options that can be followed after identifying the passion.
- At an early age, the child should be exposed to as many hobbies as possible, because his passion can be triggered out of these hobbies.

□

39

Believing in Himself

A belief is a set of ideas which a child thinks to be true. Beliefs are a set of thoughts, emotions, ideas and views a child has and believes in. The child evolves his belief system based on his perceptions and experiences which are personal, familial or societal. He gets these experiences from home, friends, school, relationships and the social environment. It may be a positive or negative belief system. A belief system is his inner-software and is basically the most important component of character. One of the best values to inculcate in the child is the value of self-belief. The grooming of a child includes not only his physical well-being but his thought system too.

Value

Self-belief is basically child's confidence in his own abilities and judgements.

Benefits of Self-belief

- It is like an inner compass which guides the child in the entire situation, be it the issue of right or wrong, good or bad.
- Believing in oneself, child can take any step without any hesitation or fear. Self-belief helps him to acquire confidence.
- It prepares him in facing the problems of life. It makes

him focus on himself rather than blaming others.
- It encourages the child to take risks and be more productive while helping him in remaining positive.

Development of Self-belief in the Child

- As a parent, your role is like that of a gardener who protects and nourishes a plant and weeds out the problems. The plant has to grow on his own.
- Before going to bed, the child should appreciate five (5) special qualities in himself, like his achievements, good deeds, talents and abilities. It will help his subconscious mind to work overnight for him in a positive way.
- The child should visualise what he wants to achieve in life. Tell him to write down the steps which he can take to achieve what he wants. Tell him to say affirmative sentences to himself to achieve what he wants and whatever he believes in, can be achieved.
- The maximum time a child spends with is his own thoughts. For him to develop his self-esteem, he must talk to himself in a positive, supportive and inspiring way.
- To demonstrate this self-belief, make him do a thing that he is afraid of, e.g. if he is scared of darkness, or to give a speech in front of others, let him reaffirm belief in himself by repeating "I can do it. I am well prepared to handle any situation." Then he should confront his fear. Not only the child, even you too will be surprised at the ease at which the fear is overcome.
- Let your child take risks, make choices, solve problems and abide by what he starts. Do not try to rescue him from each failure. Let him learn to face failures.

- Don't do everything for him. Give him work to do, however small it is, like selecting his own clothes, dealing with his friends, choosing his school.
- Do not over-praise your children. Too much praise will spoil them and make them egoistic individuals.
- As parents, you should never compare your child with other children. Every child is unique and the only competition that a child faces is with himself and not with any other child.

□

40

Value of Taking on Responsibility

The value of taking on responsibility for one's words and deeds is of paramount importance in the life of a child. This act of becoming responsible, not only helps the child to become independent, but also helps them to stand up for their actions—right or wrong. Parents are quick to come to the defence of their child and the smart child is aware of their weakness. Parents little realise their folly in such an action and end up creating brats and spoiling the future of their children.

Parents can be divided in 3 types on the basis of their outlook of life of their child. The first class of parents is destiny-oriented parents who think that whatever is happening or will happen to their child is destined and bound to happen. So, the child has little role to play except to put in efforts. There standard approach is 'The child will become what is destined!' The second types of parents are those who think that destiny has hardly any role, and with effort, child can be whatever he wishes. For them, whatever they are is the result of the choices they have made. The parents with third outlook believe that efforts have a major role but destiny too plays its own role. The child is the co-author of his destiny with destiny also playing its role. As parents, we must induct in the child that he is the product of his actions, his responses and his choices and not the result of any other thing or invisible-hand.

Habit

Responsibility means the *ability to respond in a positive manner*. Simply speaking, it means that the child must be told that whatever happens or whatever may happen, is a result of the choice or response made by him in his life.

Benefits of Taking on Responsibility

- Makes the child responsible. He realises that he is not the product of circumstances, but is the architect of the circumstance that he faces.
- Makes him 'act' instead of 'react'. If he learns that he is capable of changing the circumstance, the only option left for him is to change it, by taking action.
- Learns not to crib or complain, which is the general trend in many a child these days.
- Instead of blaming others, circumstances or situations, the child learns to tackle the situation head on.
- Helps him cope with stress, anxiety and tension. It raises his self-esteem and confidence.
- He grows up as a responsible family member and citizen.

Developing the Habit of Taking on Responsibility

- It is the general behaviour of parents, that when a kid falls down and cries, parents pretend to hit the floor to pacify them. They blame the floor, instead of explaining to the child that the fall was because of the carelessness of running on a wet floor, which caused him to slip. From an insignificant everyday incident the child is taught a negative value of blaming others for his lack of responsibility.
- Never pamper the child or allow him to blame others

for his actions. Even if he fails, let him bear the responsibility.

- Teach him to own up for his actions. When the results are beyond or below his expectation, your job as a parent is to encourage him to come forward honestly.
- Entrust small acts of responsibility to the child, like locking the home, paying phone bills, buying groceries from the neighborhood store or even paying his school fees at the school reception. Parents must stop trying to solve their problems.

□

41

Habit of Meditation

Meditation is better than medication. Modern science corroborates it. One of the key habits which parents should strive to imbibe in their children is the habit of meditation. Meditation is a way of focusing on self. Most successful persons use this power of meditation. Such are the benefits of meditation that some schools have started devoting a special period for meditation. Meditation has many forms like breathing exercise, *mantra* chanting, yoga, listening to devotional music, etc. The main type of meditation for children is loving-kindness meditation, body scan meditation, mindfulness meditation, etc.

Habit of Meditation

Meditation is a process by which we connect to our mind and soul.

Benefits of Meditation

- Reduce stress in children and controls anxiety, depression and mood swings. It promotes emotional health of the child.
- Enhances self-awareness and can boost kindness, memory and focus.
- Helps to fight any addictions, be it to mobile, TV, etc.

- Increases positive thoughts, immunity and longevity of life.
- Improves sleep and sharpens mental health.

Developing this Habit

- The first thing in the morning after the child has had his bath is to meditate. He can start by devoting just one minute. The first step is to focus on his breath. If any thought comes, let it flow and bring back the mind on the breath.
- Meditation can be very effective during the stressful periods of examinations. So, make the child do meditation for some time just to make him relax.
- Meditation can also be very effective if it is done just before sleeping. It can be accompanied by light music or a meditation song.
- There are specific breathing exercises known as *pranayama* which a child can learn and do. Meditation can also be done by chanting a *mantra*. Make him listen to one YouTube video in a week as to how to do meditation.
- Make meditation a family affair. If possible, join him for some basic meditation courses, like **Art of Living, Inner-Engineering, Sahaj yoga**, etc.

□

42

Habit of Making One Person Smile Every Day

A smile is contagious; it is like a therapy, a medicine. The best thing to give someone is to make him or her smile. It costs nothing except an exercise of face! We, as parents, must develop this unique yet simple habit in our children to make someone smile every day.

Habit

It is a random act of making someone smile every day.

Benefits of Making Someone Smile

- When a child makes someone smile, the chances of receiving a return smile in is very high. The reciprocity of a smile can make the child cheerful and positive.
- Changes the low mood of the child and also of the other person. Makes the other person happy and thankful.
- Learn the skill of appreciation and complimenting. A genuine smile can make the child seem more likable, attractive, intelligent and even trustworthy.
- Helps the child establish better social relations. Many

times it happens that the other person is just waiting for an indication of a simple smile.

Developing the Habit of Making a Person Smile

- Teach your child to appreciate what is good in others. A genuine compliment is the best way to make others happy and bring a smile on their faces.
- Teach your child to reach out to those who are in need of help. If the grandparents live away, let the child call them once in two days and ask about their well being.
- Teach your child to be courteous not only to his parents and elders but also to people who assist him in his life, like the maids, drivers and other attendants, both at school and at home.
- Do random acts of kindness, like wishing and saying thanks, helping the elderly, listening to others with care and attention, respecting everyone, etc.
- One of the best ways to inculcate this habit is to make your child give one of his own belongings to a needy person it may be clothes, items of stationary or toys.
- Even if nothing can be given, a heartfelt smile and asking about the other's well-being can bring a smile on the other person.

□

43

Value-based Learning

Simply speaking, learning is a process by which something is registered in the mind of the child. This may be a fact, a figure, an idea, an image, a value or an emotion. Our prevailing education system emphasises more on bookish facts than on values. A child is graded as intelligent on the parameters of how much he has learnt in terms of facts! His knowledge is generally equal to the number of facts he has mugged up, like what is smallest, largest, biggest, oldest, etc. No doubt, facts are necessary but only stressing on facts, which he can look up in a fraction of second on his smart-phone or a tablet, is not true learning. Causes must come before courses, which means each learning must have a reason.

Value-based Learning

Knowledge is a process of development of the potential of a child to its fullest, by bringing out the physical, mental, social, emotional and spiritual qualities inherent in him. Knowledge has two aspects: learn facts about known world by studying subjects like history, geography, maths, which tell the child what is around him; know what are values, purposes and intrinsic goals of life. For example, the school teaches about Ashoka the Great. To know when, how, what and where about Ashoka we learn the facts, but the values for which Ashoka was known is equally important. His impact on our culture and life in terms of values of *ahinsa* (non-violence) is the true knowledge about Ashoka, the great. The purpose of education is not mere mugging of facts, but creating a value system so that the child can learn how to connect these facts to a purpose.

Value

It is a process to teach the child the purpose of learning.

Benefits of Value-based Learning

- Connects his bookish knowledge with practical life. The child feels a greater sense of connectivity and belongingness. It kindles his interest in studies.
- Aims at unleashing the true potential of a child. It develops his inherent skills, values and qualities.
- Helps him understand the facts in a better way as a child can connect the facts with the purpose of knowing them.
- Aims at developing his overall personality instead of restricting him to accumulating the facts and theory.
- Helps the child to become more creative, imaginative and original thinker.

Developing Value-based Learning

- Parents should ask the child some basic questions as, what is the purpose of studies? Why study geography, maths or history? How can these subjects and their learning impact him? For example, while teaching history, parents should teach them what they have learnt through specific incidents. What is the moral behind an incident like war and other devastation? Integrate his syllabus with value-based learning.
- Teach the child to relate learning of books with his own day to day incidents in life. Teach the child to

differentiate between fact and value, fact and lie, truth and lie.

- List out the basic values like empathy, love, kindness, gratitude, honesty, etc. and choose the values you want to imbibe in the child. Teach the child as to why these values are important.
- Encourage the child to read self-help books.

□

44

Value of Success

'Success' is the most used and sought after word in the world. Everyone wants it, but only a few get it! Success means different things to different people. Success simply means reaching from where the child is to where he wants to be. It is getting what he actually desires. It is a change in the current state of affairs which may be a circumstance, person, place, thing, situation, event, etc. For example, for a kid, success may be getting a toy by convincing parents! For a child, success may mean getting a certain score in exams! It may be a student cracking the exams of IIT or medical-entrance. *For parents, it may mean successful grooming and settling their children!*

Habit

Success is the gap between what we have and what we want. It is to teach the child to reach from where we are to where we want to be.

Benefits of Value of being Successful

- The ultimate purpose in the life of a child is a life of purpose. This purpose is a destination called success. Value of success makes him find his purpose.
- Teaches him to handle failures also, because not all his activity may be successful. Success breeds self-

confidence, a sense of achievement and satisfaction in the child.

- Grows a child in inner success as well as teaches him many values of life.
- Makes him focus on himself and improve his qualities instead of competing with others.

Teaching the Habit of Success to Child

- The first step to be successful is to define what success means to the child. As per Jack Canfield, success has seven aspects, namely success in health and fitness, family-relationship, finances and monetary aspects, business, carrier and profession, personal goals and aims, enough leisure & entertainment and societal goals like giving back to society. Make your child set specific goals, like health goals that cover may weight, shape height of body, goals of school and career, like percentage or grade he will strive for, what type of career he will opt for, what is the position he wants to secure at that level, etc. Make him write his goals as detailed as possible and also write a deadline when he will achieve them, like 'I want to be fit and healthy' is an ambiguous goal, while 'I will reduce my weight from 60 kgs to 55 kgs by the last day of this year' is a specific-goal.
- Which of the above seven aspects incite the child more? The aspect which attracts him more defines his area of success. He may be good in any of them or all of them. His success is the level of progress and improvement in his areas or aspects! He may wish to be a sportsman, a doctor or engineer, having a fit and active body, follow his hobbies as profession, etc.
- Make him give ranking in a scale of 1 to 10, 10 being the highest in all the seven areas of life. Tell him to

give a score out of 10 to his present state of these seven areas each. Ask him as how he can improve upon these areas.

- Start with very small but non-competitive areas like making the child do 20 push-ups a day.
- Teach him to compete with his yesterday and ask him as how this day may be better than yesterday.
- Ask him daily for two minutes before he goes to bed as to what he wants to be in life? Ask him repeatedly. Ask him who his role model is, what are the qualities he likes in his role model, how he can be like him?

□

45

Habit of Honesty

If honesty is the best policy, shouldn't it be inculcated in life, so that it becomes second nature and remains with us throughout our life? One of the most talked about yet rarely executed value is honesty. This quality has to be ingrained in children so that it becomes a habit. It is a desirable value and unless parents 'walk the talk' themselves, the child will never learn.

Honesty

It is a value which teaches the child to be truthful to himself so that he is true to the world.

Benefits of Honesty

- The value of honesty is the basis of character and moral value. It makes the child truthful to himself as well as to his family, friends and nation.
- Helps the child to better asses himself.
- Makes the child reliable, predictable and dependable.
- Helps him develop better family values and avoid short-term benefits in life.
- Not having this value can spoil the child's character and make him unreliable and a person not to be trusted.

Teaching Honesty to the Child

- Honesty starts with small acts of not telling a lie. For example, in the popular poem, 'Johnny Johnny, yes Papa', Johnny tells a lie about eating sugar and the poem sadly ends mockingly, 'Ha! Ha! Ha!' The child should be instructed that it is wrong to tell a lie, however small or insignificant the issue is, as the lie will be found out and it would bring shame and embarrassment to him.
- Dishonesty means even the smallest of acts like telling frivolous lies, cheating during exams, gossiping about weak students etc. Sometimes, very young children, out of innocence and the urge to possess, steal anything which belongs to other children, like pen, pencils, erasers, scales etc., which are fancier or different from the one they possess. If parents find such acts they must counsel their children and teach them the true value of honesty.
- Many a time, the child manipulates truth and partially reveals the facts out of fear of punishment, for instance, older children might begin to hide their true scores/ marks especially if they happen to be low. The parents must encourage the child to accept the truth without the fear of punishment.
- A lie is a lie and we should be careful, especially in front of children. A common example is when a parent instructs the child to lie when they do not want to answer a phone call, saying that they are busy or not at home or have gone for a walk and have left the mobile at home. These small acts of lying might seem harmless but promote dishonesty.
- It is important to speak the truth in words, thoughts and actions. Parents are the child's role model. They should be extra cautious and try not to tell a lie.

They will try to reason out and say, 'If Dad/ Mum can lie then we too can lie'. Further, the parents must not speak ill about others or spread false news or rumours in front of children or even otherwise. Children will imitate what parents do.

- Reward honest responses from a child. However bitter the truth may be, it is good to encourage honesty and discourage responses that are unpalatable.
- Make a distinction between a mistake and a dishonest act. An error committed unknowingly is pardonable, but the parent has to ensure that the same mistake is not repeated. Dishonest acts must be punished, though not harshly as the child will then resort to telling lies in order to avoid unpleasant episodes.
- Teach children stories with a moral. Teach them the short-term and long-term benefits of honesty and dishonesty. In many schools today moral science and moral values instruction with examples from the lives of great leaders are told to students, so that they understand the concept of honesty.

□

46

Value of Sharing

'A friend in need is a friend indeed' defines that 'helping others' is a core human value. If we care for somebody, it's but obvious that we would share something with them, be it an idea, an opinion, or material benefit. We must have read *sharing is caring* which simply means that when a child shares something with others, it amounts to caring. It is because the child is kind and helpful that makes him think about others. To survive and to make the world a better place, helping our fellow human beings is essential.

Habit

The habit of sharing means giving a portion of what a child has.

Benefits of Sharing

- Makes the child more compassionate and kind as he tries to learn the problems or situations faced by others without actually facing them.
- Helping others has an intrinsic element of reciprocity. If our child helps someone, he is bound to get help from others.
- Makes the child responsible and acceptable.
- Makes the child happy, positive and satisfied.

- Alleviates loneliness and enhances our social lives and as per research, even helps us live longer.

Making Sharing Habit

- One of the best ways of making the child develop this habit is to make him play the role of a friend in need. Suppose we are poor and we have no clothes to wear during winter, how would we feel? Test his response by asking him his reaction. If he responds by saying that he would give away one of his best jackets, as the poor boy's need is more, we encourage the action and feel proud, knowing that our child has imbibed the right value.
- Teach the child to do an act of kindness, like helping an old person to cross the road, lending his books or games to his friends, making a stranger smile, saying thanks.
- Teach the child to say 'thank you' if he has received an act of kindness.
- By being a role-model ourselves. Do a daily act of kindness, the child observes and imbibes this habit naturally.
- Integrate kindness into the routine of the child. When we find our child trying to share, make sure we appreciate his act.
- Highlight sharing with others. Suppose a friend has shared a book with the child, praise the act of sharing by his friend.

□

47

Value of Compassion

Another personal trait of paramount importance for children is compassion. Compassion means care, consideration, concern and kindness. On a deeper level, compassion can be broken up into sympathy and empathy. Sympathy means to show concern on the sufferings and problems of others; empathy means understanding others' problems by visualising them. It is a feeling for others by placing oneself in their situation. Emotional quotient has become the number one quality that is sought after in grooming, parenting, professions, etc., apart from the intelligence factor or quotient. The pressures and demands of society have reached an all time high and only if a child is compassionate and tender hearted, can he have a chance to grow into a kind, caring and good human being.

Habit

Compassion means being kind, caring and understanding.

Benefits of Value of Compassion

- Makes the child kind, considerate and understanding.
- Helps him understand another's perspective in a positive manner.
- Nurtures in him the value of giving back, helping and caring.

- Breeds positivity in the child and he becomes a source of emotional-shelter for his friends and peers.
- Makes him a good listener and helps him develop the skill of socialising.
- Helps him win friends and influence people.
- Assists the child to be happier and spread happiness around.

How to Develop the Value of Compassion

- One way is to discuss and practice common attributes. Human beings have certain common feelings on account of being human. Every human being goes through pain and suffering when they receive a personal injury, insult, setback in their job, finances, death of a loved one, separation from a loved one and so on. Let the child play the role of a sufferer so as he can step in the shoe of the sufferer.
- Show compassion even to those who mistreat or misbehave with us. Instead of seeking revenge, the child is taught to withdraw and detach himself from feelings of negativity or angers.
- One of the ways to develop the habit of compassion is to show empathy. For example, in case you are suffering the loss of a near and dear one, try to explain to the child the fond memories that you harbour with the deceased person, the sharing of meals, ideas, conversations, family functions, gifts out of goodwill and now things will never be the same. Also, try to explain to your child how you are coping with this loss and allowing the pain and suffering to be gradually eased out of your mind.
- The child can be made to affirm that 'I am happy and in control of my feelings'; 'just like me, others too are seeking happiness, trying to cope with

sufferings, changes in different phases of life; I am compassionate to the sufferings of those around me; I can empathise with their sorrow, death, pain and suffering as if it has happened to me; I do my best to listen to those who are in need around me either by sympathising or empathising with them; I will teach my friends and classmates that it is important to be compassionate to others as we never know whose turn it could be next.

□

48

Value of Courage

One of the values that parents must cultivate in their children is courage. We call any act as courageous when a difficult act is performed despite the fear despite facing risk. Fear stunts the growth and true potential of a child. Courage is not only physical but it can be mental and emotional too. It entails stepping out of our comfort zone and allowing ourselves to get rid of our fears. For example, trying a different food, speaking up your mind, following an unusual passion or hobby, standing up for a friend, etc.

Value of Courage

It is to teach the child habit of doing something difficult yet bold.

Benefits of the value of Courage

- Makes the child bold and confident.
- Makes the child to be a risk-taker as it helps him experience both success and failure in life.
- Helps him overcome his fears and insecurities.
- Assists him to communicate effectively by expressing his thoughts, feelings, emotions fearlessly.
- Helps him to stand up for others.

Develop the Habit of Courage

- Children can be urged and encouraged to take small bold steps, to take calculated risks, especially when parents are there to closely protect and build a safety net against possible failures.
- Children should be praised when they perform a courageous deed. Stand by him, as overcome the risks involved.
- Challenge children to get out of their comfort zone of playing safe, especially in their choice of careers and encourage them to explore the unknown paths.
- Set an example, so that your child can emulate your courageous deeds and decisions. If you want your child to be brave, you have to be brave first.
- Teach courage by narrating to children stories of valour. Shivaji's mother Jijabai used to describe at great length the heroic deeds of persons who carved their names in history. This helped Shivaji develop an attitude of courage and strengthen his mental and emotional make-up. Let the child learn through role play, that is they can enact the life history of Rani Laxmibai, Prithvi Raj Chauhan, Ranjit Singh to name a few. Another alternative is to make children watch biographical movies so that they can emulate the brave warriors of yesteryears.
- Encourage the child to join NCC in school.

□

49

Habit of Humour

'Laughter is the best medicine' and is more effective than an apple in keeping the doctor at bay. This positive habit of taking things lightly and valuing humour even in the most difficult of situations is a good habit to inculcate. Humour is an attractive quality and children should be encouraged to laugh and also make others laugh. Medical research corroborates the fact that humour or laughter is the best therapy for life-stress. Such is the importance of laughter that in India there is one branch of yoga which is known as laughter yoga. People install 'laughing Buddha' just to bring positivity in their homes. One of the most viewed programmes on Indian television is 'The Laughter Challenge'.

Habit

It is a habit to take things lightly and add humour to life.

Benefits

- It helps child fight low-moods. It makes the child positive.
- De-stresses the child and it helps him to face even the low events of life in a light manner. It will help him to be disease-free and increase his immunity.
- As per Ayurveda, thoughts of a person influence him

the most. So if the core value is humour, the child will remain happy, healthy and vibrant.

- Makes the child more creative and develop a presence of mind as he tries to create humour out of a normal event.
- Brings positivity in him and also spreads positivity around him. It increases productivity as well as the receptive power of the child.
- Helps in better learning and memorising as the best thing a child remembers is what amuses or surprises him.
- Makes him more social and thus win more friends.

Developing this Habit

- Make the child read and learn a joke every week. Give him a book of jokes to read and this way, he will learn 52 jokes in a year which he can use in any situation.
- Make him write a joke on any situation and also make him to find positivity in any situation. Make him identify funny qualities in others.
- Try teaching him his syllabus in a funny manner.
- Be an example first by bump humorous yourself so that your child learns from you.

□

50

Value of Reward Instead of Bribe

The twin most used tools of parenting are 'bribe' and 'reward'. One of the most common habits which parents unknowingly impart to their children and which are easily imbibed by children is the habit of bribing. Bribing means giving the child what he asks for in lieu of what the parents want him to do. There is a subtle yet qualitative difference between bribe and reward. Bribe is a negative step made out of desperation by parents and which generally aims at stopping a bad behaviour of the child. It is a short-term step which gives immediate benefit to the parents and also imparts instant gratification to the child. On the other hand, reward is a positive step which aims at promoting the child to do what is in his long-term benefit. For example, if a child insists that he will eat food only if he gets a mobile and parents comply, it is a bribe. On the other hand, reward is giving him a dessert on his eating healthy food.

Value of Reward over Bribing

It is a recommended practice for good behaviour of a child to be promoted through reward instead of surrendering to their demand.

What are the benefits of reward in lieu of bribe?

- Bribe breeds negative emotions and makes the child feel powerful, whereas a reward makes the child feel proud as he has earned something. Bribe makes the child feel that he is dominant while reward makes him feel proud and happy.

- Bribe spoils the child while reward prepares him for the future. Bribe gives him a feeling of plenty and a habit of refusal from parents. This is a negative tool in parenting. Reward brings the best out of a child.
- Bribe gives instant gratification to the child and makes him selfish. He develops a 'give and take' relationship with parents. Reward develops him into a selfless and loving child who develops the habit of gaining out of pain. A bribe is a temporary tool which is de-motivating but works on urges, whereas a reward is a motivating and permanent tool.
- Bribe is 'if-then' while reward is now-that!

How to Develop the Habit of Reward in Lieu of Bribe

- Make parenting value-based instead of object based. The purpose of parenting is not to give children undue comfort but teach them what life means. Do not succumb to tantrums, emotional blackmail or pressure of the child out of love and affection or out of desperation.
- If the child has already developed that habit, start telling 'no' to small and insignificant incidents of bribes.
- Discuss in detail with the child about the long-term benefits and disadvantages of instant gratification.
- Give rewards which are intrinsic, like values, by encouraging a child or by praising his good qualities, etc. Show appreciation of good work instead of giving any material thing. For example, if a child insists that he will go to school only if he gets a mobile and parents comply, it becomes a bribe. On the other hand, reward is in giving him a bike on getting good grades in his exams.

□

51

The Value of Handling Failure

One of the most important habits without which all other habits or values will be ineffective is the value of teaching your child, the art of handling failures. A successful person climbs many a step, experiences failure, rises up and again attempts to climb the ladder, till he learns the art of handling failure. It is very rare to find a successful person who has not met with failure.

Meaning of Failure

Simply speaking, failure is the fine line between any expectation and its result or outcome. Failure can be absolute as well as relative. Suppose a child does not qualify in an exam by scoring the minimum qualifying marks, he is termed as a failure. In other scenario, suppose a child expects to get 90 per cent marks but gets only 80 per cent, it is perceived as failure by 10 per cent, in relation to his own expectations, or his friend or the topper who may have scored a higher percentage than him. Trials and failures are a part of life of a successful human being.

Value

It is teaching failure as just a step towards success.

Benefits of the Value of Handling Failures

- Equips the child to handle stress and failures.

- Prepares the child to face the world in a better way.
- Teaches him to handle both failure and success in life to become a balanced child.
- Reduces his attachment to results and makes him more focused on action and process.
- Save the child from negative tendencies, like depression, frustration or extreme steps like suicide etc.

Developing the Value of Handling Failure

- Every person has a story of failure prior to becoming successful. Narrate your own personal story of failures and teach the child on ways to overcome them.
- Teach the child that both success and failure are perceived realities. They are two sides of the same coin. None can reach anywhere without experiencing the process and journey which passes through failure and successes.
- If he has failed in one field, ask him to list out the reasons. Also, if he secure a good result, ask him to reason out the steps taken and find out what was missing in the field where he failed.
- Failure is not failure if the child has learnt from that failure. Failure is failure only when he has failed to get up.
- Show the child a good movie which teaches the value of failure for instances, 'Karate Kid'. Teach him that failure is not the end but a means to success, be it delayed.
- Make him read self-help books so that he can learn the value of failure in making his icon succeed.

□

52

Habit of Gifting

(Habit of Giving Your One Belonging Each Day)

It is better to give than to receive, says the old adage. As per a Harvard University research, gifting others puts a bigger smile on your face than buying things for yourself. Gifting is one of the most effective habits of personal development. It is a very simple yet highly rewarding habit which gives an altogether different approach to life and the way children possess their goods, belongings, things, items and articles.

The Habit

It is an act of giving up one's belonging and gifting it to others or someone who needs it. It could be either gifting a new thing or giving the things which the child already uses.

Benefits of Gifting

- Makes the child less attached to material-things and dissuade him from indulging in mindless possessiveness. It makes the child internally happy and blissful.
- Helps the needy, thereby making the child serve the society. It cultivates the twin feelings of 'giving up' and develops the habit of altruism.
- Helps the child in de-cluttering by getting rid of the

unused stuff. It may save money for buying gifts on occasions, make better user of goods and things and be a better shopper by buying what is required and not superficial stuff.

- Helps the child to strike good relationships and earn friends.

Cultivating this Habit?

- Children who are privileged with plenty, possess extra things extras or which they do not require. Let these things be used as gifts to give to the needy in a positive way that brings mutual happiness.
- Before the child goes to sleep, make him select one of his belongings, which can be anything, and put it in a polythene bag. This bag can be used for creating a 'bag of kindness'. The belonging may range from a very small article like pen, comb, shirt, T-shirt, clothing, unused diary, book, toy, pair of shoes, etc., to a not so small article like an extra bicycle. After a week or so, make him choose a day and people to whom these belongings can be gifted.
- Many parents make this act of gifting on a special day, like a birthday or before any festival or New Year. Keep in mind that only one belonging (item) per day is selected and resist from selecting more than one item so that it becomes a habit.

□□□